T0196422

To The Abyss

And How We Lost Touch with Spiritual Living

Dr Michael A. Gray

Author of:
"Spirituality: Key to Physical and Mental Well-Being"
And
"Spiritual Health Inventory Scores and Abstinence" (a dissertation)

WESTBOW®
PRESS
A DIVISION OF THOMAS NELSON
& ZONDERVAN

WestBow Press books may be ordered through booksellers or by contacting:

WestBow Press
A Division of Thomas Nelson & Zondervan
1663 Liberty Drive
Bloomington, IN 47403
www.westbowpress.com
1 (866) 928-1240

Because of the dynamic nature of the Internet, any web addresses or links contained in this book may have changed since publication and may no longer be valid. The views expressed in this work are solely those of the author and do not necessarily reflect the views of the publisher, and the publisher hereby disclaims any responsibility for them.

Any people depicted in stock imagery provided by Thinkstock are models, and such images are being used for illustrative purposes only. Certain stock imagery © Thinkstock.

ISBN: 978-1-4908-5967-5 (sc)
ISBN: 978-1-4908-5969-9 (hc)
ISBN: 978-1-4908-5968-2 (e)

Library of Congress Control Number: 2014920136

Printed in the United States of America.

WestBow Press rev. date: 11/18/2014

Acknowledgements

This book is to those who taught, modeled, and provided honorable examples during an earlier age. Then, one was known by their actions and beliefs rather than a media promotional. I miss the time when things were simpler and somewhat more respectful being based upon an ethical, genteel spirit. Specifically, this work is provided based upon the values and beliefs of a family lineage that defends the infinite relevance of God to our existence. His authority over our lives and the obligation for us to make an ongoing effort to remain compliant to his guidance is our family reality. Our worldly purpose is to serve his creation.

From the results of reported family research, English Tudor-era rulers from whom I have descended exercised leadership that relied on our Creator's plan for guidance. Their precept for governance served as a primary, honored obligation directing their behavior while they acted in service of others. This basis of leadership demonstrated a humble character and recognized that our humanness required accepting the superiority of our Creator. Later, a major enlightenment era family ancestor penned the ideas that we are free to live with liberty and possessed inalienable rights from God. These beliefs are expressed in America's founding documents as a central premise for the implementation of our government. I add to my heritage's contributions in writing of the dire need for active recognition of God's authority. We are expected to complying with his rules should we wish to ensure survival and prosperity. This opposes present-day preference of the created self-perception of self as god. Disregarding our source will seal our fate, I suppose.

Later, as my family worked the soil and tamed the wilderness in the Shenandoah Valley of Virginia as early settlers (without government subsidy), we continued to observe scripturally-sound principles. We approach daily life with a respect and attempted obedience to our Creator even now. At present, a poisoning effect from some is expressed as an intentional, deliberate indifference to our Creator. Failure to obey his instructions or embrace his practices has placed us at a point of realizing our mutual destruction. Further, their presentation is smug and indifferent to the serious nature of our social crisis. This is our world. Meanwhile, they often present with ignorance of the cause-effect impact from their behaviors. The frequent counter is disdain for our expressed concern, disrespect of our heritage, while debasing us with immorality not becoming of a civilized people. Thus, while I attempt to honor my past, I ask you to consider our future.

It bears noting that I have arrived at the place to write this book from an extensive amount of college-based education with over 17 years of study and 4+ completed degree studies. I believe that I am thereby a meagerly qualified, yet competent student of human behavior. I include doctorate-level education of a psychologist to sharpen my insight. This insight has also developed additionally by serving others for over 20 years to address life issues and mental health concerns on a routine, daily basis. However, the qualification that best serve this project is based on the experience of a like number of years reading, studying, and applying scriptures to everyday life. This is at the core of my understanding while providing the basis for my thinking.

As a servant that was provided a minimal amount of talents, I have determined that the master's interests are best served by using the gift of his talents provided me to publish this book. The goal is to advance his kingdom. The true test of the 100 fold increase will be found in the number of those who will take advantage of this material to reach the place of gaining our Lord's acceptance. From this mindset I offer my humble thoughts and considerations for the benefit of our rescue by our Creator. I pray that my fears go unrealized and hope we alter our future course.

Dedication

To all of those who do more than simply believe; but
also do great works for the glory of God and the Son.
To those who have faith that they will be found worthy
having put themselves last, they will be first.

Preface

The title is such that it is intended to require people to acknowledge our present living guidelines as essentially flawed and insufficient. Society appears to have a somewhat less than acceptable status in relationship to our Creator. An observed, central premise is that many people live for the present with the satisfaction of hedonistic, pleasurable objectives as a central focus for their daily lives. If it feels good then do it is the mantra that is at the source of the behaviors for these individuals. Further, the fundamental problem remains that, for a vast majority of the population, they don't demonstrate a knowledge, care, or reasonable consideration of their Creator's expressed plan. Instead, God is seen as the innocent babe (or a doting elder) rather than as the one who will rule with an iron rod. The common perception is that spiritual individuals must suffer every injustice and experience every insult without a whimper. Their actions suggest that it is preferable to live carefree and only make amends when facing their death.

I accept, realistically, that many people understand that much of what I address has not fundamentally changed over time. Nor is it likely that those considered will alter their course soon. The despondent or the lazy must be motivated to work and those considering terminating a pregnancy must be faced with the reality of the consequences from such an extreme decision. Certainly amoral behavior is an insult to cultured people and is never in vogue. It is entirely the case that constant media attention of every adverse, severely offensive crime and malaise to society makes us immune and desensitized from this ceaseless, sensory overload. And, conversely, it may very well be the case that things really are as bad as perceived by those of us who have seen the full extent of change that have occurred. The key factor to consider as one reads this book is to consider the cumulative effect that has occurred by the many ways and means we have discarded the design provided for appropriate living found in God's plan. This effect has led to a presently inadequate, and fundamentally amoral, lifestyle that is opposite of God's intentions. This idea serves as the primary theme addressed throughout the book. To me, it is relevant to define what has happened as being basically rebellious in nature and is demonstrated in many significant instances.

A psychological concept known as "frame of reference" must be considered so that some will not offer a rebuttal to my concerns as being inconsistent with how things "really are". The concept is primarily a means of expressing (as it regards a consideration of this material) the timeline that we each have individually lived within. It serves as the basis for our way of realizing change, continuity, and allows for comparison of various parts of our lives. If you are born in the 1990's, that is where you would begin your comparison against. However, if you were born in 1950's, the difference from that time to the present is much more pronounced. And, as some of my oldest family members can attest, the present is so lacking when put in comparison to their youth that it is truly troubling. So as to avoid the tendency for a "halo effect" that results in an overly generous valuing of our youth (the good old days), I recognize that we were not fully aware of the full extent of the evil that existed. However, things are truly worse and let there be no doubt. There continues to be many acts of kindness, love, compassion, and humor which allows each of us to live each day and provides evidence to us and our God that we still are redeemable-the basis for our survival has potential. The perceived problem is that the present hidden evil has overtaken the principles, values, and humble ideals which gave us connection to our Creator. Further, those who wish us ill and those who disrespect our heritage (and God) are having their worldview serving as the basis from which we operate as a society. Clearly stated, evil is often calling the shots.

A proof reader stated, after reviewing this book, that she believed that this book expressed anger. I, therefore, felt it pertinent to address her concerns. Yes, what I have observed is distressing and I believe that my angst is justified due to a perceived disregard for everything that our Creator wishes for us. In spite of his provision, a growing number of individuals blatantly disobey him. Throughout the total sum of our existence, many continue to demonstrate a blissful ignorance and noncompliant behavior towards his expectations, while initially innocent, has become intentional. This does not mean that there are not those who value him with obedience. Instead, the number of those who disrespect him, as well as the degree to which they are disobedient, has increased to a point when it must be addressed. He has demonstrated his loyalty to us and loved us since we first came on the planet. Meanwhile, civilization has increased its rebellious nature beyond justification (as is argued throughout this book). There continues to be an on-going, and ever-expanding, separation between ourselves and our Creator.

I continually demonstrate shortcomings in my walk with God and his Son due to my humanness. Yet, I have an appreciation and love for them because they provides for my best interests. This love for them requires me to be loyal and do what I know is expected of me. I am obligated to support and defend them (if only in my meager ability to do so) while they protects me in daily life. As a mental health professional, I engage in therapy with clients to deal with their thoughts, feelings, and behaviors. We collaborate to come to an understanding of what they are doing and is it serving their needs and interests. If not, what should they do or how should they think, feel, and act? At some point that varies depending on the client, they "get it". As you look at them, their eyes light up and an emotional expression occurs signaling that they have reached a point of understanding that relate to them in a deeply personal, human way. This is what I want for the reader of this book to experience. I pray that an understanding of their need and obligation to recognize God in a deeply personal, human way occurs. He is our father, and in spite of our behaviors, he loves us dearly as does the Son who sacrificed himself for us. Yet even now, we continue to be noncompliant. We will honor and please both the Father and the Son more than we can ever imagine if we honor their instructions and return that love along with our obedience. Even if those efforts only expressed in our errant, human manner.

This book's purpose is not to register a litany of charges nor constitute a list of complaints regarding how we have changed from an earlier time. Rather, I intend to cause others to consider gaining a personal acceptance that previously held beliefs and practices forwarded by our Creator are timeless, universal, and truly beneficial. These previously held beliefs are not open to modification by any age due to failure to behave coming from a personal choice lacking in insight about our Creator's ways. I can readily acknowledge that things have progressed (although that is not an appropriate descriptive term for what has occurred) to a point that is impossible to justify. We are, therefore, in a compromised position that we cannot defend. At this point there is cause for the alarm to be sounded and for a call to action by anyone who is concerned for the continuity of humankind into the future. This work is, by no means, neglecting that there are many wonderful, decent, respectful people who honor the Creator. They are obedient and compliant of his ways. Instead, as only a drop of oil in a vat of water pollutes it, we are approaching a dire state due to our indifference to our responsibility to be vigilant in our compliance of our Creator's plan. You can only dilute a thing to a certain degree when it has lost its flavor and is rendered useless. It is not a stretch to consider this principle when speaking of our future potential.

The real irony is that, although the substance of this work is of importance to the future of many, they will "fiddle while Rome burned". This is due to a failure to recognize an immediate need to live in accordance to a spiritual standard. Such standards allows for development of fulfilling and enriching qualities which will ensure their eternal place as a favorable one. To those who feel led by the spirit of God rather than by the flesh desires of man; I offer this treatment of spiritual living. I humbly pray that this book will serve as an awakening and as an insightful chronology of our decline so as to head off further regressions. This text is for those who sincerely need their Creator's involvement in their life. The truth is, we can't afford to pay the cost for our spiritual malaise and need to take advantage of this period of grace while it is still available. Let me be quite clear, I don't see myself as somehow above a need to consistently seek the Creator and, as a sinner, I do fail on many occasions. However, I keep him actively on my mind and continually in my deliberations.

This work is designed to offer an attempt to serve others as much while irritating the mind with a view point that is both controversial, yet scripturally-sound. I do not believe that some will fully (or fundamentally) support the positions offered inside. Scriptures points to the fact that there are those who will travel the well-worn path that leads to their fall. Likewise, those who travel the path leading to God's eternal blessings and share a like-minded spiritual position- they will find support in reading this book. Yet, it would behoove anyone to read this material and ponder it carefully. It would be a grave error to casually discard it as a traditional, conservative, and/or right-wing attitude. I only hope that you will benefit and profit from the insight available from the reading. As such, this book is not based on a Republican or a Democratic politically-based position. Rather, it is a call from one who feels as though he is in the wilderness and is expressing his concern for our survival as a nation and as a civilization that was made by, and under, God's direction and authority.

How do I know if anyone will invest their resources to purchase or take time to read and study this work? In actuality, I don't know that this will be the case. However, if one only endeavored to engage in the (writing) exercise based upon a certainty that it would be well-received, it would be the case that much of civilization's trove of achievements would not have occurred. There is a certain amount of uncertainty when beginning any enterprise. I cannot let this hinder me as it is apparent to me that I am responsible for leaving a legacy. This legacy includes being a good steward of my life as well as making a good-faith effort to be obedient to my Creator. I am encouraged to add something of substance towards a promotion of his kingdom here on earth during my lifetime. As scripture states, if one is spared and enters the kingdom (who would otherwise not be spared) then, there is rejoicing. It is with this thought in mind that I do this thing.

A dear friend of mine told me as I prepared this work that it was entirely possible that I was doing the writing of this book to serve the purpose of assisting me to grow in my walk with my God. It is certainly the case that many ideas have become crystallized within my concept of the state of the species since I began to do this work. I have been provided with meta-cognitive (thinking about thinking) processes that allow me to assess my opinions and measure the accuracy of those previously-held beliefs. Some of what I thought has been fine-tuned or altered to account for a more robust, complex understanding of how things interrelate. This helps to understand how we have arrived at the point of our present predicament. Nevertheless, the central and abiding precepts that I hold come from scripture. They have not been dismissed by my participation in human-based educational pursuits or in deference to man-made theories and models. Frequently, they fail to account for the primary core causes that led to our problems regarding survival. Things are really simple, we only try to make them complicated in order to allow us to see ourselves as complicated, sophisticated, and entitled to amend his instructions. This leads to seemingly ignorant, poorly-founded attitudes that appear to only confuse rather than simply live by the guidelines established by our Creator. Rather, it would wise to keep things manageable based upon God's reality rather than our own.

At the present time I find myself stating to those that I come in contact with who are also in the same generation as my own self (or of an even earlier one) that this is not my America, and certainly not my world. They understand what I mean. Those ideals that shaped our development and we accepted to be right behavior are now gone. In actuality, there appears to be little apparent understanding of those previous ideals by more recent generations. As a child, I was taught that one acted according to the golden rule in their dealing with others, truth always won out in the end over evil, and doing the right thing was not a slogan. Instead, it was the way we approached living each day. Today, many in the world act based on the primary consideration being what is in their self-interest with the environment being manipulated to that best interest. This is also without meaningful consideration that also includes the interests of others. Further, the size of the wallet and exploits in the bedroom serve as the yardstick to determine the status of the individual. No longer is it relevant to have a primary consideration for ethics as the basis for behavior as it is merely a code established that frequently is twisted by whatever way possible in order to frustrate any attempt at accountability.

Finally, it seems only appropriate to acknowledge that each generation has a challenge as we continue to further distance ourselves from the Creator's design for the species continued existence. In spite of this we have managed to continue to the present time; or so it is surmised. Therefore, the argument of secular, hedonistic segments of our society is that we will not terminally falter in the near future. In their eyes, we are actually improving and realizing a fuller potential. This is in spite of the accumulated insolence which constitutes our categorical indifference to our Creator. Unfortunately, it seems that we are at a critical juncture when we will correct ourselves by acknowledging our heritage and spiritual origins. Or, we will go so far astray so as to lower ourselves to the point of immorality that approaches the times of the later Roman Empire. That may not be a concern for many who blissfully avoid any consideration of the future. Regardless, it is to their peril that they allow such a potential outcome. Due to a lack of consideration beyond what scriptures describes as a vapor (our life on the planet, here and then quickly gone), eternity has been ignored due to the universally acknowledged, humanistic principle of being in the moment. The result is a drive for immediate gratification rather than considering life in the future after we depart our mortal bodies. This may very well be the crux of the matter when attempting to understand humankind's folly. As for me and my house, we will serve the Lord.

Contents

Introduction

It was an evening at twilight during a warm, June night when I experienced an awakening during the time while my uncle was speaking a blessing over me on his front porch. Granted, I was aware of the stories of Jesus Christ and of the prophets as presented in the Holy Scriptures as a child-the truth was, I hadn't really experienced the presence of my Creator on a personal, intimate level until then. From that time forward, things have never been the same. In spite of educational advancements and other aspects of development that typically take one far from a spiritual plane, I have continued to grow and nurture my personal relationship with my source as I have moving forward.

Just previous to this event, I began working at a facility where there were many spiritual individuals whom I observed on a daily basis at the organization. Without exception, they were generous, kind, caring, and compassionate individuals who demonstrated a general, positive personal regard for others and honored the rights of all. They were not short and abrupt with others, provided love to others regardless of whether they share their views, and had a tendency to see everything with a positive, upbeat lens. In short, over time I began to feel that I wanted to present myself in a manner that mirrored the behavior that they showed for others, based on their inherently decent perspective.

Now, with many years having past, I find that I continue to struggle with the ability to portray these qualities and traits that so enticed me to seek out a spiritual existence. It is not an easy road and many times I feel as though I have fallen short. Perhaps it is a central issue of deciding when strict observance of God's guidance is preferred or when it is more appropriate to have patience so as to allow others to grow with the hope that they will find their way. The challenge to identify what, and when, to use either is central to functioning appropriately as a spiritual being (or so it seems).

There are many things that just are; they don't need a discourse and flexible thought process to come to a conclusion. The commandments and pronouncements found in scripture are absolutes; they do not fit into a flexible mindset and are constant in all situations and in all times. Conversely, there are themes of love, compassion, nonjudgmental-based behavior that speak to flexible thinking that takes into account the circumstances and human frailty when coming to what is the right, spiritually-appropriate way of acting. This book addresses both areas of thought; I hope that I have done so in a frank, honest manner while not ignoring or watering down in any fashion that which I have been taught by scriptures and the efforts of a number of very spiritually-sound individuals.

In the final analysis, God knows our hearts and from that well-spring we shall be seen as either acceptable or lacking. Staying true to central beliefs from a conservative, traditional upbringing leads me to conclude that what is enclosed is not for everyone; in fact, at the present time with the prevalence of secular society that borders on mockery of our Creator, it may not even speak to most people. Let there be no doubt however, that it does speak to what scripture and faith have forwarded over time in the development of my thinking. It is not always necessary to be new and improved, just steady and steadfast to principles that have come before us and will keep us safe in their observation.

Lastly, I am a fan of people in general and, despite having anger over much of what people do, I still love them as a creation of our God. I enjoy them and wish for their best in all cases-God is not an individual respecter of person and loves each of us deeply. I wish that they may prosper and have abundance and that they may come to know their Creator on a deeply personal and meaningful basis. I do not wish for any ill to others, regardless of their worldview, lifestyle, or design for living. Instead, I sincerely pray that they may come to acknowledge the rightness of living as a child of God in obedience to his word.

Only upon completion of the time allotted to us to live will he hold us accountable and, meanwhile, every opportunity is extended to each of us while we are alive in our fleshly bodies to be grafted into our Creator's heavenly kingdom. My very personal, and painful, fear centers on the reality that many will suffer in an unimaginable manner due to the unremitted avoidance of developing a special relationship with God and the Son. They will ultimately fall into a depth of the abyss that is described in the end of scripture-this is personally painful for me to visualize. I do not gain any pleasure from pointing out others indiscretions nor realize any profit from highlighting the deteriorated conditions of our times. Further, failure to address our world means to me that I have failed to care enough to reach out to all people as I feel obligated to do. I believe that my Creator expects and requires this of me as his servant. Further, we must live as a co-habitat where everyone's best interests must be considered (within the context of remaining obedient and compliant) while our Father looks out over all of his creations. May the joy of serving the Lord be realized by all of his creation to ensure their ultimate benefit and allow for their best interests being served?

Chapter One

Base Needs and Simple Fulfillment

When Is Enough- Enough?

As a young child growing up in the rural, northwestern part of Virginia I didn't have a whole lot. To me it was not a little bit and I was content. According to what society suggests nowadays however, it wasn't a lot. I had a nice warm house to live in and plenty of food to eat although it was rarely ever steak. When I reached 14, I began working during the summers and after classes during school sessions to earn whatever I wanted. My father worked in the unions as a carpenter while my mother managed the household quite well as a full-time house manager. My brothers, and I, attended the local public school system that was graded as exceptional for public education in Virginia. After graduation from high school, I joined the military to gain a trade and adult stability. The government was not involved in my upbringing nor was subsidies or welfare in the house. There were times when work was called off for my father due to winter weather or because of labor strikes. Yet, due to exceptional financial management of our resources by my mother during the times of plenty, we were assured of being able to weather the occasional economic downturn when these challenges occurred.

No one told me that I was poor (or that I was entitled to anything other than a chance to participate in the American dream), rather, I was expected to be the source of my own success or failure. I learned from my father that one had to go where the work was, not sit at home and lament the poor circumstances of a lack of readily available work. Even though it meant a 120+ mile commute to get to and from work, my father saw to it that we did not go without because that's what fathers did when I was a child. All of these aspects of my years living with my parents have left an indelible imprint on me as to the responsibilities and roles within the family, and, what it means to be part of a family.

As will be frequently mentioned, marketing has suggested (subliminally and otherwise) to the public that they must have what they are selling. If we don't have these things, we are in some way fundamental way operating with a general lacking. The automobiles of our parent's day were less expensive (even before inflation) and got us to where we wanted to go. The car just didn't have a sunroof or built-in video and audio players. We didn't have gourmet meals that were prepared by any major processed food supplier and available for purchase at the local grocer nor an overpriced (and less than nutritious) meal from the local fast-food restaurant. (However, I don't understand why it is called fast-food when you may wait 10 minutes at the window for your order that may be absent what you paid for). We ate at mom's kitchen and we got what she decided to be nutritionally sound instead of pizza or hamburgers with fries. We got what we needed as a person to survive as well as an evening snack to spoil us. There were no dumb questions as whatever we wondered about would be addressed by our parents to the best of their ability. Proper language was expected with respect for our parents always being afforded to them. (To this day I couldn't imagine thinking, much less speaking an obscenity towards my parents).

Even in my earliest days (as a 7 year old), I was acquainted with the stories of Jesus and of the religious tenets associated with the Protestant faith. I read the stories of the Bible and attended Sunday school and Sunday service as a young child. The impact of these experiences has been profound and has served me through many times as a young adult to deal with challenges and obstacles that have, and continue to occur. Between these experiences, as well as my upbringing in my parent's home, I did not assume that I had to possess multiple, material items in order to be considered successful (or sufficient) as an adult. Early on in life, I learned a valid principle in dealing with life. If it doesn't matter in 5 years from now, then just let it go. If I have to have something, be something, or do something within the context of those parameters then I would attempt to succeed, otherwise, just don't sweat it.

Since I also learned at an early age the value of work, I realized that if I wanted something then I would have to work to earn it. Expecting others to provide what I needed was unheard of. How could I expect the government to cater to my whims…if I really needed it then I better get busy to be about securing it through my own means and efforts. Besides, based upon my upbringing, God would provide a way if I was meant to have it. Neither me, nor my classmates and friends, had designer jeans, high priced sneakers, or authentic major league apparel. Levi pants and jackets were in. As long as our clothes were clean (and did not have holes in them), we were good to go. Our parents never quarreled in our presence, maybe an occasional glance of annoyance between them, but they kept their disagreements to themselves in the privacy of their personal time.

People went to bed at a reasonable hour in our house so that they could be up soon after the sun made its appearance in the morning sky. We did not tolerate making fun of others because of any rationale; we were more concerned about our own appearance and deportment rather than focusing on others. My father often told me that it didn't matter as much what clothes I wore as much as that I was clean (in his day water was free and soap was never in short supply). Another significant understanding that I receive from my father was found in his statement that "there is never enough time to do something but always enough time to do it over once you have screwed it up. Do it right the first time and take the time necessary to do it so or don't waste your time and the time of others by failure to do it right". Even though I, as well as most other classmates, encountered mistakes and missteps we learned together that an appreciation for each other is what would be the key to gaining acceptance while in school, and also in life. After completing my high school education, and having received many examples modeled to show what an honorable and genteel behavior consisted of from many accomplished, traditionalist families in the area, I entered the United States Air Force as an enlisted, airman basic.

I am proud to say that I was afforded the opportunity to have served with true gentlemen who demonstrated what professionalism consisted of during my years in the military service. Although it was during the time of armed conflict (Vietnam), I was spared from having the experience of combat and of the misfortune of being wounded or worse. My supervisors, command-staff officers for a majority of my total enlisted length, took me into their confidence as in the same manner as a Christian accepts a stranger into their home. Further, I was made to feel that I was valued to the same degree as if I were their own child. Thus, I was afforded the needed support while entering adulthood. They were kind, patient, caring, and demonstrated a self-felt need to guide my development while instilling in me a work-ethic that was polished while recognizing the need to be personally responsible. Also, I learned of the appropriate manner of behaving in a way that acknowledged my personal accountable for my work product. I was able to develop pride in myself and also grow due to the available support wherein I felt appreciated and respected as a member of the military-serving my country in the tradition of my family that went back to the days of Valley Forge. As I look back on this portion of my life, I can only hope that today's GIs are afforded the same experience that I was fortunate to have had. After the completion of my military service, I attended college for what was to be the first of many degrees that include each available level of college education. My military training equipped me well in my approach to my education in a mature manner (effectively also) and, minus that military experience, I do not wish to consider how I would done with regards to my collegiate efforts.

I earned a portion of my college assistance through the G.I. Bill while the remaining educational pursuits were addressed personally. I took on a primary financial responsibility in order to attain over 17 years of college education and 4+ degrees. My father had always harped to me throughout my upbringing that "you can be anything that you put your mind to as long as you put out the effort and take the time in order to achieve". And, you know, he was right. This statement had propelled me throughout each challenge and served to motivate me to provide the effort necessary to succeed. This is advice that every young person should be told as well as sharing the lessons associated with this concept that make it relevant to their efforts to be productive. In many cases, I have found that the younger generations do not demonstrate that they have been provided with this very fundamental insight and personal understanding.

After a time of discovering myself and realizing what my obligations were in society, (and coming to understand many nuances associated with being a productive adult), I met my wife through our shared association with a local hospital. We made certain that we were the right one for each other's best interests by taking time to develop a relationship based upon friendship, respect, and mutual consideration. The relationship was not based solely on physical attraction (not saying that I was not smitten with her also), and due to being prepared, we have been able to see the union through during our lifetimes rather than being unprepared for the various trials associated with an intimate partnership. It was important that we have similar conservative, rural backgrounds so as to mesh as a couple. We have depended upon our faith in Christ and the Father to push ahead through each challenge that has come up during our life together. God and the Son are first, everyone else second, and ourselves, last; and that is the way that life best unfolds because we will always be provided for if we don't leave others out of the bounty of our lives. I can be thankful that, for the most part, we have been healthy and provided for without significant, debilitating illnesses as of this writing.

Now, well into adult years, I have significantly more than I would have thought possible or than what my parents had during the same age span. God has provided for each contingency as it occurs and having faith in his ability to fulfill those needs hasn't wavered throughout my life. He has provided in ways and in instances when it did not seem possible, much less likely, that the emergencies would be positively addressed. And the chief principle that has allowed me to lead a satisfied life free of resentment and distress is having a realistic expectation of what is needed and required to live satisfactorily in God's grace. It is not about the unending pursuit of things, rather with the continued nurturing of a satisfying relationship with God. Demonstrating a true compassion and concern for our fellow human beings while allowing God to continue to amaze me with his unending blessings and favor has been the result.

It is a central concern in addressing the issues covered in this book as they relate to the principle of what is enough of what is "need" and what is "want". Many confuse the two and interchange these two terms consistently. I was raised to understand that unless it is absolutely essential for our survival and longevity then it is a "want" and not a "need". Food we need, shelter we need, water we need, the ability to manage our hygiene on a base level is preferred, and freedom from fear is essential to function effectively. Other than the satisfaction of base needs, it is a "want" and we need to be observant that we should carefully approach the satisfaction of the want. The adage that one needs to "be careful what you ask for" is relevant and those things that we want may prove to be not in our best interests. The idea that, if it is a good idea today then it will still be a good idea next week is relevant to discernment as to the relative necessity of our wants being satisfied.

I was always impressed with the idea that it is disrespectful to ask for our wants unless we had been prudent, for the most part, and did not continually clamor for attention to satisfy what are wishes were. I maintain the belief in adulthood that God is responsible for addressing the needs of the entire planet and he doesn't have time to listen to an incessant demand for stuff. He sees to it that I am not hungry, that I have a warm or cold place to live in (dependent on the needs of the season), and that I am pleasantly disposed to my surroundings. He provides me with employment and good health and I feel good about my eternal disembarking location. That is plenty, but God provides even more.

So the question becomes, what is enough? A person needs the basic deficit needs as well as the ability to be part of something bigger than itself. They needs to be nurtured by a close, loving unit of individuals who are associated by blood, common interest, or mutual affinity and may be led by a common goal in the midst of sometimes difficult, challenging circumstances. What is troubling is that clothes that cover the body are not enough for many now days. Instead, they must have a label that is suggestive of a designer or repute by marketing firms and advertised as being the thing that we must have. The food we have must be more than to allow for pleasurable subsistence; it must be from a national chain of restaurants that are advertised by popular media outlets.

Our homes must be large, have many amenities that include multiple bathrooms with spa features, a play and game room, studies for the adults as well as for the kids, and multiple car garages. The homes must allow for the individuality of the family members and further the present-day tendency to avoid close family relationships by an excess of space that also requires never ending hours at the office to pay for it. This often further alienates each other by lack of closeness. Being in debt is not helpful…it is infinitely more appropriate to live a stress free and well-adjusted life that is directed towards a relationship with the Creator. As it is written, a person cannot serve two masters; and at present, the service of the debt has forsaken the reality of having a meaningful, personal relationship with the Creator.

In asking the question as to what is enough, it is worthy to also consider the overarching drive of humans to find pleasure as a means of defining what enough is. It takes on many divergent pursuits by people such as sex, drugs, sports, music and entertainment, video, games, television, shopping, and the list goes on and on. The overriding objective seems to be finding satisfaction with what we own, what we feel, and where we are in our lifetime. When our needs relating to these (and other) pursuits have been met then we have enough at that moment. However, this is only temporarily as tomorrow the pursuit begins anew for something else. The only thing that I have found in this life that is all encompassing and fulfilling without need for further supplication and amendment is to have a truly satisfying and noble relationship with our Creator. This is the essence of enough and the real tragedy is that people spend a lifetime in the pursuit of things and chasing dreams while ignoring the truly self-completion found in such a relationship.

It is not about having your own way or not experiencing the feeling of being embarrassed or challenged in your thinking. Often there is a sick feeling when we realize that we didn't measure up and that is to be expected. The hardest thing to accept is that our actions are not always (or even usually) going to be above the criticism by others with the frequent feelings of personal inadequacy. The main thing is we keep trying, and when we have those moments when we feel that we have done right, we need to be spiritual enough to give the Creator the credit. After all, he is usually the one who made everything happen for us. This is part of the process whereby we are held in amazement of his glory and we marvel at these moments as to his ability to do not only the right thing, but the perfect thing for that time and circumstance. Having this experience is more than enough.

It is enough to have been provided the right guidelines with which to live as well as to entertain all of the experiences that occur during a lifetime. It is enough to feel peace and contentment with a personal acceptance that things will be okay. And, even when things get bad, the support to go on is always present and on time. It is more than enough to feel and know that you are loved and cared for and that even though God is the most powerful being in the universe he will stoop to your level. He will share in your joy and sorrow, provide guidance while not being harsh and unwieldy, will allow for enough slack for you to learn and discover the limits to our competencies and abilities, yet allow us to grow and reach the stars. Meanwhile, he gives us the knowledge that he did it for us and with us we walked through the journey together. He even cared enough for us to be amongst us in order to walk a mile in our shoes so that he could understand life from the human perspective. It suffices that I am not alone and he sticks closer than a brother to me. With this relationship I fear no man and know that I have the ultimate "big brother" who can put anyone who attempts to harm me. That is a blessing that cannot be overestimated. And, conversely, he is kind yet firm in his admonishments to me when I am out of line and fall short. He teaches, guides, loves, directs, and encourages my every effort while gently nudging me onward to bigger and better things. That is enough.

Chapter Two

Considering Humanity

An Attempt to Understand Our Frail State

A central impression that one may gather from reading this book is that I may have a poor opinion of humanity. This assumption is not true or appropriate to understand my view of my fellow human. My expectations, and frequent subsequent disappointments, served as the basis of an inner conflict within my personality and a subsequent ongoing battle to be fair and considerate. I am aware of the peculiarities associated with our human condition based on a spiritual development and from education as a mental health professional. Yet, I am irritated by the behaviors that imply a disregard for our Creator due to their lack of consideration for his wishes. Further, a vast number of my fellow inhabitants routinely demonstrate examples of ignorance as a frequent, human practice. The best way I can address this ongoing battle to be tolerant and avoid drawing negative conclusions about my fellow man can be explained by my reasoning regarding the common experience of driving on the road. Most will be able to associate driving a car and the inherent daily challenges for a positive acceptance of our fellow human.

Getting to where we intend to go when driving involves observing the traffic signs, acknowledging others on the highway, and navigating through various situations that could be fatal if not addressed competently. Reality is that we are frequently aggravated by others who fail to behave as we believe they should. We can be often irritated by seemingly ignorant acts that others do on the highway. Frequently, I draw the conclusion that, if they can't even drive the posted speed limit while riding my bumper instead, they either are ignorant or disrespectful of my rights as a human. Further, if they are unwilling or unable to do this simple thing of being in compliance with the speed limit signs, then they certainly aren't able to be respectful and obedient of the Creator (thus their eternal state is doomed). That ends with my determination being that they probably will find themselves on the outside looking in when the day of accounting takes place. They will have difficulty justifying their efforts to their God. However, there are, as I have already stated, other things to consider which I have been made aware of during my professional training (as well as being based on age and spiritual experience) that are important to add to drawing a more well-reasoned conclusion. These considerations should give pause when considering the behaviors of others and in forming opinions about those who share the road with me.

An initial consideration to take into account, when thinking about the person who has demonstrated the irritating driving habits, is their age. An older individual has diminished reflexes and cognitive insults as a result of wear and tear on the various regions of the brain that perform functions that are needed to operate at a high level. (Driving slow and appearing to be overcautious is not a defect, it is normal for their age). A younger individual has not had the full development of some regions of the brain associated with inhibition while not having reached a state of understanding of their mortality. Their understanding does not include the reality that they won't live forever and they could die if they screw up. This lack of development (until the age of 25, or thereabouts according to some literature) serves to be demonstrated in erratic and aggressive actions that may be dangerous for others, as well as themselves. (This is the primary reason that their insurance premiums are higher, as a group, than older drivers). Further evidence of youthful aggressive impatience is associated with brain wave pattern that lead to high stimulation resulting in quick, frequently not fully-assessed behaviors. In neither of these instances are these individuals really irresponsible or immoral and functioning in a generally disrespect attitude. They are only acting in a manner that their developmental state provides them, ability-wise, to respond. However, we usually do not reserve a favorable opinion for these groups. Frequently, we often express obscene responses as communication preferences to them. This supposes that we fail to consider the individual beyond our own limited labeling of their behavior as being stupid. It would indeed more spiritual to make an attempt to take into account what is interfering with their attempts to do what we would consider appropriate.

Next, it is important to consider IQ (intelligence quotient) as a factor in the behavior of others. The figures vary based upon what source you use, however, on average the statistics suggest that over half of the population operate at a normal/average level (for lack of a better means of description). They are able to function appropriately regarding activities of daily life on the whole. The stage of reasoning that they have achieved may not be beyond the theorized third stage which is known as concrete-operational stage in some instances. This means that they may not be able to handle problems consistently in a sufficient way that is able to identify complicated and somewhat subtle, obscure elements. Doing so would allow one to make considerations that would result with a novel solution. This does not mean that they are significantly deficient. If one asks the question as to what God requires from us, I would believe that this level of intellectual sophistication is sufficient to be compliant and obedient to his instructions, absent any need for a more advanced IQ score. However, the mercy of the Creator is needed in many instances due to the undeveloped state of intelligence, failure to use that intelligence, and our human frailty that results in ill-advised, sinful acts.

Continuing, there is a portion of the population that is in a mild, moderate, severe, or profoundly affected IQ range. I feel that God does not hold them to the same standards that he has for others. It is not their fault for this circumstance and the love of our Creator for them is such that, in my estimation, that they are assured of favor and necessary considerations from a merciful God. I have addressed all of these factors in order to forward the understanding of the frail nature of humankind. I also state that we are not of any less, or any more, value in our Creator's eyes based upon what category we fall into. To those who have been afforded a superior IQ, much is expected to be demonstrated for the benefit for others and that is the added responsibility that they have to live up to. This is due to the scriptural adage that for those that much is given much is expected. Yet, we are all equal in the eyes of God who, scripture states, is not a respecter of person-instead he loves all of us equally.

With due deference to a circumstance that is at the core of some instances of misconduct, it bears noting that physical and mental illness are at fault for poor behavior in some instances. Having worked in a hospital setting, I am able to have seen instances when the sheer experiencing of pain is such that the individual should not be expected to uphold a high level of standards in conduct or to the same extent of accountability as those not afflicted. Although it seems theoretically possible to believe that we, as adults, should meet minimal standards, pain often leaves us with a form of emotional expression which does not allow for a well-reasoned response. These individual are to be afforded our compassion and provided with our efforts to mitigate or minimize their suffering. This is more appropriate than making comment of their lack of conformity to standards of conduct which we deem reasonable and appropriate. This is a situation when our understanding for our fellow human involves being considerate while recognizing what they are experiencing within their state of suffering. However, this is not always readily considered.

For a brief moment, I make a qualification as it relates to all that follows. Scripture claims that, to everything there is a season. Without any doubt humans can be very funny, precious, caring, loving, decent, and worthy of both our Creator's and of our individual, personal well-wishes and acknowledged valuing. This is not in question; what must be realized that this book is written in the spirit of a season requiring our obligation to be aware or the reality that our innocent characteristics are not sufficient for failure to realize our situation as serious, the clock is ticking, and God cannot be expected to continue to tolerate our behaviors, both individually and as a civilization. So, as we consider humanity, know that I acknowledge our goodness and realize that there are many who are doing what they are being expected to do by our source. It is the evil, the degree to which it has increased, and the severity of its expression that is the cause for serious concerns for the state of humanity. We are each personally, as well as collectively, responsible to take into account our hindrances and effectively address those concerns.

If we are able to consider all of these hindrances to humankind and attempt to demonstrate a moral, spiritual approach to our lives, it is reasonable that our Creator has acted for our sustainability. His allowances for misdeed require an acceptance, love, and loyalty to his Son as an avenue to avert paying the full costs for our sinful deeds. Knowing this, he made our compliance with him based upon basic understanding skills to avoid confusion. It is my belief that we have an instinctual knowledge of God and of his wishes without a full education on the subject. However, the intelligence that we use to be obedient to him comes from knowing his expectations for us regarding our conduct to others, to him, and as individuals learned early on. It began as children, required learning traditional values and beliefs, and demonstrating an application of scriptural instructions. Often, this began with Sunday school classes or instructions from our elders with a resultant awareness and wisdom forming our foundation to build our lives on. This spiritual way of viewing life was provided by more spiritually-developed individuals who give us instructions for the necessary base of knowledge required to know God's expectations as obedient children. When one knows the principles of scripture and values from our countries founding, they are able to function effectively. And, having been assisted during their development to refine spiritual beliefs and practices, they approach life issues and daily circumstances with the principles for action coming from this knowledge and training. This is the essence of what is called spiritual intelligence. The central problem that permeates present-day society is that spiritual intelligence is frequently not developed, therefore, decisions and behaviors come from somewhere else. Absent the Creator, secular-progressive humanistic-originated values are used in order to fill the void left by the absence of God.

Beginning in the 1950's, science and beliefs based upon the humanistic movement began to make inroads into the educational, social, and cultural lives of western civilization. The very nature of intrusion of these institutions was in opposition to previously held ideals and beliefs with the unanticipated results being a promotion of man as the source of their world instead of God. Faith and a dependence on God, in practice, essentially ended for many men as they began considering themselves as enough to master their environment without any other assistance. The idea developed that we can "know" how, why, and by what means that everything exists was perceived as possible with the use of science. Science, in essence, became the new religion. A reliance of science led to the consequences of the demise of faith which was based on an idea that we did not know but must depend on our Creator without a full understanding of life. Now, it was believed we know and, then, we can make the world to be as we wish by our own devices. Meanwhile, being "in the moment" (which supported immediate gratification instead of long-term commitment) took the place of considering eternity. (Not only was there a failure to consider our long-term future, the impact included a lost skill of patience). If the future is not considered, then any importance of an obligation to be compliant to our Creator ceases. Having "unconditional positive personal regard" was a misrepresentation of the scriptural principles. It represented a snippet being absent the full contextual scriptural principles, yet it was the new social expectation as a reasonable human. (As a general consideration it seems hard to accept that those who rape, molest, murder, or steal from someone will receive this theorized acceptance from those victimized). Common sense does not appear relative for this new humanistic expression of right conduct. The outcome was the end of accountability. This new reality replaced the notion that, as kids we make allowances for poor choices, but in adulthood the lessons are expected to have been learned.

Beginning then, and with increasing difficult thereafter, social situations allowing exposure to things that developed spiritual intelligence were banned, legislated against, or deemed archaic and discarded. (The absence of traditional Judeo-Christian guidance such as disappearance of the 10 Commandments from public buildings, ending of religious practices such as prayer in school, and responses to atheist-originated complaints leading to constitutional case decisions adverse to God's instructions are but some of the most obvious examples). And, it is in no small consideration, the dwindling church attendance and, preference for entertainment to take the place of this attendance in religious settings or moments of solitude to consider our origins and the Creator is where many are at now and represents an end result to this transformation.

To bring the point home in a more personal way consider that there was a time not so long ago when people did not have the daily distractions like television or radio. Before then, people actually talked with each other to make use of their spare time or read to expand their minds (typically the Bible in many instances). This verbal exercise was usually such that it aided in an extensive development of language. As such, they could express exactly what they thought in a complex use and application of English to reach a deep level of connectedness during conversation. Further, the rules of logical thought and principles associated with critical-thinking had been refined and regularly practiced as well.

Then, beginning in the early 50's signaled the introduction of media with an unintended result being that these practices initially diminished and, later, became virtually nonexistent for an ever increasing number of people. The media industry introduced the concept of air time (sound bites) and getting your marketing message out meant that you had to use a phrase or catchy word which made the hearer conjure up an image. Though brief, it was designed to mean a more significant idea. (Since advertising was expensive only a few seconds could be afforded to make your point). Instead of developing a thought with critical thinking and logic and development of an argument, a word was given an undeserved value (denoting emotional interpretations instead or developed rational thinking).

Further, this has led to giving a label to others to describe them, instead of considerate and thoughtful expression of the sum understanding of another person based on reasoning. This has resulted, in effect, dumbing down language use and ignoring employing reasoning to arrive at thoughtful conclusions. Further, this has also resulted in a great reduction in the use of serious discourse. The preference is now for a shallow, and often inaccurate, representation of reality. This is how we have "progressed" which I counter is a lack of adequate use of thoughts and a replacement of thoughts to arrive at making decisions (higher level process). Instead, emotions and feelings form the basis for decisions that routinely affect lives, often negatively. The preoccupation with pleasure, feelings, and emotion formed a perceptual triad for new social thinking which frequently excluded a contribution of a rational content. This is not good.

Operating based on emotion requires fundamentally very little from us. We just are, or so seems the most simple of ways to define it as a basis of functioning. Essentially, people just prefer to not experience troubling emotions and will do what is necessary to avoid considering why, instead of what, they are feeling. Only when we think do we do that which serves as the literal basis for a higher state than mere animals; the ability to reason. Since we have dumbed down our behaviors and frequently operate absent any nurturing exercise of critical thinking (preferring feelings) we are actually planting the seeds to our own regression. This does not advance the interests for improving our condition.

It is my observation that a discussion about people words and actions, the weather, or our work week experiences have taken a significant majority of our time without fulfilling our obligations as our brother's keeper. Only a few minutes of attention to the news daily would inform us that Christians are being beheaded, cancer continues to be a scourge, and poor-parenting is a severe impact on our problems. A large number of our society follows the pattern of, fundamentally ignoring our ever increasing distress with a simple response of, "pass the coleslaw" while distress, death, and disease ravage our hopes and potential. Certainly, when we experience loss and painful disappointments we may only be able to function in that moment with emotional expression. However, our definition as human beings requires being understood by a realization that rational thought and critical thinking exclude utterances such as "what's up dude" or "what's happening" serving as deep, meaningful, or insightful personal expression.

As a means of highlighting the seemingly innocent, yet profoundly serious consequences for basing behavior and choice on the dependence on emotion rather than employing rational thought, let me provide the following. When we feel stressed and edgy (a feeling), a potential consequence is that one begins a habit of smoking cigarettes. In other instances of emotional pain, and in attempts to avoid the painful experience, many turn to abuse of drugs as a solution. This is a primary result of present-day consideration of emotion and a response based on the consideration of feelings, instead of considering the reason that cause the feelings. If we felt a specific way and we considered why we felt that way, we could benefit by understanding the value of the emotional experience to our growth and develop inner strength. This seem logical to me.

How was making decisions from emotional reasoning that ended in addiction or, decades later when we develop lung cancer from smoking, make any sense? This strategy for decision making is not defensible to arrive at a plan? How is that use of emotion to determine conduct working for the person then? I believe my point is self-evident. Essentially, the suggestion seems to be that experiencing any emotional pain or discomfort is to be avoided without consideration that this state can be an opportunity for growth and development if realized, assessed with rational thought, and redirected with an appropriate reasoned solution instead of an emotion related action.

To further extend the consideration of present-day preference for emotion over reason, consider the difference between what we consider truth versus spin. Or stated another way, an explanation for the difference between objective reality and subjective reality represents a different way to approach the same issue. A spin represents backward thinking. We have a position that is often based on emotion reasoning and must, therefore, tailor our explanations or perception of facts and reality to support and forward that favored position. We, in effect, have an opinion and must use the situation to promote our opinion or so the use of spin actually accomplishes this within its practice. In effect, it is primarily a subjective reality and is not usually based on truth (rather, it is interpretations formed to reinforce our beliefs or position).

Conversely, I find that God is essentially the epitome of truth. His beliefs or positions are, by their very nature, objective reality. The human use of a subjective explanation is based on a desire to achieve what one wants, supports, or prefers often times. When we don't let the chips fall where they may by being grounded with accurate insight (absent personal opinions) we are operating based on spin or subjective reality. The result is that a pursuit of an advantage that is not usually reasonable to consider as appropriate occurs. This serves as the actual motivation for the spin. My position is that, when reason is used (the essence of objective reality) we are more often able to deal with life in a considerably more effective manner. This is in comparison to subjective reality that has its origins from opinions, beliefs, or strategies (emotional context) versus objective reality (truth). Now, how one feels as an emotional contextual perspective (subjective) is considered acceptable and truth as expressed by a Creator is ignored. In order to face the issue squarely consider this. Fundamentally, we judge others based on their actions (behaviors) rather than their words. I have not met people who were deliberately saying that the objective reality of the Creator or his Son is wrong. In reality, the actions of society suggest that man's subjective reality is superior to the truth (objective reality) of our Creator. Essentially, our source is basically wrong. To ensure being clear on this point, our laws give honor to our Creator's misgivings and prohibitions and this is without any argument true. In spite of human behavior that is totally unsupportable, God provides us with allowances in spite of our demonstrated disrespectful nature.

Taking our basic human nature into consideration, it seems appropriate to understand that there are general constraints on the human. The fact remains that we have been flawed and inherently defective since the debacle in the Garden of Eden due to our demonstrated sin against God's instructions. This has led me to the further understanding that humans are not capable of being in total, uninterrupted connectedness with our Creator. It is essentially a result of a limited attention span capacity. This appears to be due to the interference brought on by the previously expressed defects due to the fall from grace. Instead, frequently there is an on-going tendency to avoid an active spiritual relationship due to a preference for pleasure and material comfort. More often, we function on a level that is primarily flesh-oriented rather than spiritually-oriented in practice. Due to the preeminence of science and humanism for many, the flesh-oriented portion (hedonistic and materialistic) of the present human experience has taken over most of the existential expression (faith) by people. This is at the source of my concern and basis for my belief of the presently expressed, generally rebellious nature against God. A world absent the preeminence of God and with our acceptance of the role of servant (human) without need of the master, essentially, is of little use to the Creator.

In spite of the reluctance to develop or practice spiritual intelligence we can still, instinctually, understand some basic spiritual ideals. They have their basis from right-reason and are so fundamental to our being that intense consideration and long-term training are not required. It seems basic to me that we:

- Accept that we are responsible for taking care of ourselves and not being dependent on others to do so.
- God gave us all talents, skills, and abilities and it is our obligation to use them for the benefit of others as well as ourselves out of respect for him.
- We must give an accounting of ourselves-did we give love to others and did we try to be compliant with him while taking into consideration the needs and interests of others as well as ourselves when we acted while alive.
- Come to a state of being where we have a personal relationship with our Creator and his Son that is based upon our subservient

nature to him and are observant of his commandments, guidance, instructions, and plan for our lives.

- Love everyone (as well as God and the Son) as the central focus of our existence. If we love the Father and Son a testimony to that love is obedience.
- Be fruitful and multiply.
- Leave the world in a better state than when we arrived on the earth.
- Be a good steward of our resources and demonstrate an ongoing respect for the Creator who provided us with everything in the universe.
- The family is the basic building block of society and from which all else rests as a civilization and this building block has to have the functional ability to reproduce itself or it is not in keeping with God's design.
- Everyone is equal, no ethnic group deserves special consideration or to have their identity serve as the basis for detrimental treatment. Only when we reach the point when we realize that we do not deserve special attention or consideration will we be able to live based upon character rather than privilege.

I am sure that others will not fully agree or accept what I believe to be the fundamental, instinctual understand that all humankind shares. What I have expressed serves as the basis for my beliefs, and others may have a different set of ideals. However, it seems that these ideals are generally seen by most as being appropriate, or at least, basic and general start points to the foundation that makes up the headings and sub-headings with which to order their spiritual intelligence for their daily existence. As I have said, and will address throughout this book, these fundamental principles and ideals are presently being ignored.

The perceived lack of connectedness with the Creator has led to the present-day alternative that consists of an allegiance to science and humanism, absent the preeminence of our God. This is the primary issue which has compelled me to write this book. God as well as his Son (our master) is first, all of our brothers and sisters that make up civilization are second, while we ourselves are last. This is the order that narcissistic self-interest has forgotten.

There is one other worthy thing to consider (at the higher degree of the consideration of humankind). This is essential in order to really understand our God and what will, essentially, serve to determine what will be our place after death. The functional basis of the human existence is to see, smell, taste, hear, and feel our environment and react (or act) so as to preserve our safety and provide for our needs, as well as wants, if possible. This requires us to make use of these senses to determine how to behave on a second-by-second, minute-by-minute, etc. basis and we must necessarily make "snap decisions" or, as stated in reference to professional decisions, "based on all available information" come to what is the best course of action. Usually this is arrived at, with regard to basic issues, within seconds, minutes, or other finite measurements of short spaces of time. Fundamentally, if we considered everything within our environment individually in an extensive, comprehensive fashion we would be overwhelmed with the sheer enormity of what must be understood and considered. In other words, such extreme consideration of everything would make us literally crazy. This represents a fundamental difference between us and our Creator.

From the human standpoint, a significant injury to our civilization and the lands that we inhabit has resulted due to an inability to fully realize our world. The fact is that those inventions and gadgets we have seen as progress result in destruction and environmental injury that critically influencing our potential to survive left unchecked. Simply stated, we do not demonstrate the capacity to make application of cause-effect in considering our potential improvements and, years later, experience the full extent of destructive to our environment. The damaging effects from our advancement were never realized. Our errant understanding does not provide us the intellectual capacity to fully appreciate the effects of our devices. These advancements are often fraught with problems we are unable to predict, realize, or process until many years later. Then, we are exposed to the ramifications for our inherent human inability to forecast that seemed too good to be true, actually was just that. Our Creator knew from the onset of life the dangers that we are oblivious to yet we suggest that these improvements are proof of a superior nature. We use this advancement as a means of supporting our present desire for ease and comfort but fail to appreciate that the temporal advantage may have long-term consequence. These may not even in the future be fully realized. This is but a brief example of but one means of laying bear our demonstrated lack of reverence for a superior mind of our source. Our arrogance as having achieved something of merit was not sufficiently considered; further evidence of our functional imperfection.

God is not only able to see everything in the entire universe in a comprehensive and exact detail to its most finite measure, he is able to do so without taking away from his awareness of the sum total of the universe. That is well beyond our ability to even process intellectually. Further, simply stated, he does not miss a beat. So, when I say that what determines where we will spend eternity is based on our heart which God knows, I am suggesting he knows us in a comprehensive, complete manner that allows him to consider us fairly, honorably, ethically, and to a degree that we can't even understand. Breaking it down to the lowest common denominator, he knows us in a deeply human way since he also came down to live with us and walk in our shoes to feel our feeling, know our pains, share our joys, understand our perspective, and experience so many subtle nuances that make up the human existence.

What is my personal goal in life is not only to be obedient and, even though I will continually fail, keep trying to my end. And even more important and essential consideration in order to be compliant with God's expectations, (while trying to behave in a manner consistent with his modeled behavior for my observation and mimicking) is to first, be tolerant and quick to forgive, and, further be slow to anger. In short, I need to know my fellow brother and sister (without regard for anything such as country, race, gender, etc.) in a deeply human way and be able to fully appreciate what their life is about. As I have learned, and must continually consider (although being human I many times fail to consider), is that people don't really form their opinion of you because of what you know, have accomplished, or what level of status you hold. What really matters is that you care about them and that care is demonstrated in a deeply personal, human way. This is at the core of what allows us to live out the creed that God has established for us.

Clearly and simply stated, he has given us his expectations of how we are to behave. And, this fundamentally expresses these expectations as best I am able to elaborate. These instructions are for all people throughout the world regardless if you live in Chile, Germany, or South Carolina. It really doesn't change the obligation to listen to his instructions or allow us act in an alternate way towards others. The expectation remains that we are all his children and equally responsible to obey. This does not allow us to behave in a way that minimizes what he expects as being acceptable. Further, and what is really irritating to me is, the ignorant statements of those who say "this is the modern days and we don't do things that way now because this is not the last century". In their simple way of considering their world this may be a potential point of consideration, however, his guidance was not provided based upon a certain timeframe. Trying to excuse his instructions with the excuse that they don't fit modern-day trends, is a recipe for doom. His rules are timeless and equally applicable to the total continuum of civilization. He will only tolerate for so long our irrational and illogical reasoning. It is apparent that we must pause, consider the rebellious nature that we have behaved on many levels, come to our senses, and rededicate ourselves to our Creator. Otherwise, realizing that our demise is within reach is expedient.

As a way of sharing what I feel is necessary and pertinent to my attempt to advance the discussion of an expectation for us to place God first in order to survive as a civilization the question is asked. It is one that everyone must answer for themselves. As a conclusion coming from my belief of self-purpose, I feel that my primary obligation is to serve God by actually doing something due to the gifts he has, and continues, to give. Is it enough to merely live on the planet and enjoy the resources that have been provided by God and only do those things that allow for our survival? Or, are we required to do something noble to support our Creator going beyond church attendance and mere words? Acting with his interests as my primary goal, instead of mouthing that we believe, seems rather clear. For me, whether it be from an awareness based on IQ, whether it come from an active thinking, an instinctual state of reality, or from some unconscious guidance-if I only talk the talk but don't act on a love for my source, then I have failed to count. I believe that God wants us all to count for something. Otherwise, as I have been told, we will fall for anything.

In concluding this chapter I have been thinking of how I can most clearly and appropriately give example to bring home the gist of this bit of understanding. Consider how we have essentially changed in our daily dealings with others. This represents a flagrant example of the difference in behavior that is expressed with spiritual intelligence from an earlier time versus the present, secular and humanistic way of behaving. Specifically, when I was a young person if we treated someone wrong we felt bad. In our gut instincts, knew we had to apologize and make every reasonable effort to make things right for the person who had been wronged. It could be embarrassing and was a hard pill to swallow that we were acting wrong. However, we knew that we were being watched by our Creator and, should we fail to do the right thing, then we would pay a price. The golden rule mattered and that was the essential reality that we must behave in accordance with.

Fast forward to see the common practices that are used in management and business now. The bottom line is the amount of money that you have and the goal is to continue to get more; the duty to be honorable is often not a consideration. Instead, gaining an advantage is looked upon by the person who has that advantage as a matter of being skilled and competent rather than a fair, equitable exchange. Rather than considering that character is the basis for business dealings, having the best lawyers and prolonging the controversy for as long as possible (increasing the suffering and discomfort of the other party) is seen as a smart business practice. And if you can frustrate someone sufficiently then they will give up or settle for a small amount that does not begin to reflect the amount of injury that they have endured. Further, if you can find an obscure fact, law, or evidence that will allow you to form a defense that is based on cunning and deceit; if it allows you to prevail over others then it is acceptable (called being "slick"). And, in the most obscene degree, having more money allows to bleed the opponent of all of their capital which they use for their legal defense thereby destroying them, essentially-even though they were wronged and deserving of being treated well. This is fundamentally the difference between acting based on spiritual intelligence or on present-day secular, humanistic principles. Compliance and obedience to God's law has been replaced by hedonism, materialism, and a generally narcissistic satisfaction of self-absent appropriate consideration for other's rights to be treated with respect and honorable conduct. It really does not get any simpler than that.

And, if that is not sufficient to drive the point home, consider this as further evidence of how our world has changed. I was told as a young store clerk that the customer is always right and that we must be as helpful as is possible when they ask for service. Now, when a product which you paid an obscene amount of money for breaks down, you must call someone and wait to be answered off of a "cue" list. This takes a great deal of time in order to be answered. Meanwhile, you are irritated by an ongoing use of the hold time to try to sell you something else rather than address how to fix what you have already paid for. Then, after being on hold- time you are answered with the invariable response that you have contacted the "wrong" department. You must be transferred to a wait list to be on hold for an additional period of time to be put in contact with the "right" people. Once you are answered the customer service technician asks questions that are typically not related directly to your interest, yet, serve their needs instead. Finally, you are often told that what you want will cost you an additional amount of money and you must be placed on a schedule. The point of this explanation is to show that the sheer greed of business, on so many levels, is epidemic. Their staffing reflects a desire to expand profits while not having sufficient people available so that you are not forced to wait, that having a product that is doing what it is intended to do may require additional fees separate from the actual purchase that you made, and that there exists a fundamental absence of independence of the employee to try to "fix" things. Nowadays, someone reads from a prompt card as their responses to you and do not demonstrate any clue of the frustration that the customer on the other end of the line has just spent an important portion of their day with absolutely nothing to show for it. They have been forced to listen to the companies requests for additional purchases based on their phone, hold-time advertising. This seems to me to be utterly insane!

Chapter Three

What is Not Important?

A Review of the Present State of Spiritual Affairs

We live in an age of information and practically everything that happens is, in some way discussed as the subject of idle speculation by humanity. What we do with this overload of information determines the basis of our mood, perspective, and availability of time. Too many people spend their time involved in an assessment of our peer's actions rather than on personal concerns that are of paramount importance to their well-being. I will elaborate and ask you to consider this:

Your friends do not need to know what you are doing for significant amounts of the day (or what you think, in fact they probably don't care for the most part). They are too involved with managing their own day although this fact is lost on a sizable portion of the populace that utilizes social media as a part of their daily activities. The number of those who use this media is staggering and continuing to grow although the majority of those who do are primarily teenage and earlier adults (there are other age groups represented however). And this is the tip of the proverbial iceberg with the information technology dissemination.

When I look on my email account there is significant amounts of readily available information considered to be news worthy. Invariably, there are sites that provide the user with what a movie actor or actress wore, how it looked on them, if other celebrities wore the same or similar outfit, who looked better in the event that multiple individuals did, etc. What I wonder is, "Who cares?" Do people really have concern for this trivial and useless information? What the average person needs to consider is the source. This is media self-promoting itself as being important, unfortunately many people buy into the self-serving presentations of media which advances the activities of those in the entertainment industry. For myself, I do not understand the logic associated with placing importance on people who play or pretend while, ever-frequently, failing to incorporate spiritual-based, moral lessons within their product. Further, if being physically appealing is what is important, what does that say for the one who expects attention based on looks or is popular primarily because of their body? And this leads me to a significant point about what matters?

What sustains the body, nurtures the body and mind, and allows the human being to exist is essential and the initial consideration for what is inherently important. Of that consideration, the question naturally follows as to what is the definition of sustenance, nurturing, and constitutes an existence. Is it merely the act of breathing and processing nutrients while allowing for time to rest and refurbish the cellular structure? Or is it something much more? And how much more makes up what is important? These are the questions that have been at the core of much philosophical discussion since the beginning of time regarding what is the purpose of life and what is the meaning of living? As has been stated that a lack of examination of our lives is tantamount to not living, it follows that life is on various levels and plains of existence with each contributing to the experience of having existed.

The human must function and this is at the operational level of existence. The deficit needs as suggested by Maslow are at the core of this functioning basis. The need for air, water, food, heat (or coolness), safety and security, shelter, and clothing cannot be ignored in a general discussion of what is important. Other needs such as the need for being socially connected, love that allows for a sense of belonging, and the ability to achieve something personally important to the continuance of the species is likewise important. Those things that lead to the continuance include the production of food and products to support survival needs. To these things it is important to add the process of ensuring the operation of the species absent physical and mental pain with practices such as medicine, physical health, and mental health services and research that culminates with products and entities devoted to caring for humankind.

It would be inappropriate to suggest that the concept of work is non-spiritual or of minimal concern to leading a spiritual existence. The idea of being engaged in work that was prescribed as a response to breaking God's instructions while in the Garden of Eden is something that has been the curse for humankind since that initial time of the dawn of civilization. It supports the concept of being self-reliant, industrious, and productive. Engaging in work serves as a means of measuring our worth by themselves and others with regards to being a useful member of society. It is a measure of intrinsic value to the Creator as one who honors the commitment to account for oneself and one's use of their lifetime. Work may be stated as one of the most spiritual aspects to our being. Therefore, the opposite to work is dependency that is usually not spiritual as well as often being based upon a spirit of nonconformity to the Creator's instructions. I perceive our Creator as viewing our use of personal gifts of physical and mental skills to be self-sufficient as proof of our value to his grand design. It can be said that a person's life will not work until they do.

What we do as work is important from both a developmental basis and as a self-maintenance basis. Essentially, we must work to retain healthy physical and mental functioning while we grow in our understanding of life and of our fellow people through work. It stands to reason that the resources that have been provided by the Creator must be harvested to allow for shelter, food and sustenance, clothing, etc. and therefore are worthy manners of providing work for the services of others. As such one is engaged in social connectedness as a servant, a necessary precondition to leading a spiritual life (service of others). The development and continuation of those things which allow the human race to exist and flourish are likewise within the theme of service to others; highly spiritual qualities. Farming, animal husbandry, construction, rehabilitation services, education, etc. are but the primary (albeit not total listing) of those aspects of life that follow in the tradition of services to others.

A caveat is the excessive, obsessive nature of appearance and those things that society has promoted towards this end. Vanity is not of a spiritual plane and serves to separate the created from the Creator (who is certainly not superficial). As such, beauty aids and products are nonessential to the continuance of the species and, although some may argue that extreme deformity needs attention, most beauty aids are only superficial supports for shallow living. In these instances it seems that appearances are suggested to be more important than the substance of reason, what is in the heart of the person, and the objective reality of facts. It has become so inappropriate that the present generations of teenagers and young adults rely upon a product that I, as a child, enjoyed once water was added and it was refrigerated for a time to quench our thirst on hot, summer days. What results is a visually exotic, unnatural hair color that occurs frequently in conjunction with equally bizarre (by previous conservative standards) uses of tongue, ear, belly, etc. (and anywhere else that one cares to imagine for the most part) piercings and tattoo art works. Although I am not privy to the exact place in scripture that this type of behavior is mentioned in I am, nevertheless, aware through having read a passage concerning avoiding self-adornment. It seems appropriate to consider that there exists a self-felt apparent dissatisfaction with the appearance that one was given by their Creator if changes or additions are perceived as necessary. Although expressed generally in negative manner, it is truly sad to realize that those who do so are probably unaware of the scriptural text on this subject. This seems to support what scripture suggests concerning that many will be "lost" due to lack of knowledge in the latter days. (Just a seemingly minor example yet, nevertheless, telling of our society).

With the interest of following up on the point of using self as a canvas being somehow showing a lack of appreciation for God's gift; let me offer this. Various cultures value body shapes and types differently and have opposite preferences. In western culture, thin is preferred to being fat which is considered something that is often not a majority choice. There are negative beliefs about those who are seen as fat and it is often believed that they either eat too much, too often, or exhibit poor self-control over food consumption. Besides being an ignorant manner to determine actual worth, there are often other factors that should be involved in our attitude towards others body shape. When my thyroid began malfunctioning a few years back, I found out real quick (after gaining almost 40 pounds in 3 months) that connecting being overweight to food consumption isn't totally accurate. It is wrong to misjudge those who may be considered fat as an appropriate attitude since there are multiple possible reasons for this body type.

Further, I have learned a while earlier in my spiritual walk that each and every person is beautiful in some way. With some there are more ways than others (if one is indeed shallow and primarily concerned with superficial aspects of appearance only). It may be the person's ears, eyes, hair, limbs, etc. (you get the picture) but we are all beautiful so; why must we do these unnatural things to ourselves as if that will make us into something more that we already are. We are beautiful in the eyes of the one who made us. Lastly, our true beauty comes from inside so being concerned with outward appearance is a poorly-considered approach to the reality that we are already a work of beauty. If God appreciates us then we should be good with that and not have any additional worries or need to try to improve on perfection. Concern about our appearance is but one of many unnecessary worries by humans and coming to an understanding of what is truly significant serves as a topic that many never truly resolve satisfactorily.

Working with clients in the mental health field provides me with the opportunity to guide them in a self-discovery as to what truly is important. I generally use what I refer to as a stress inoculation strategy plan to approach this topic of addressing importance for their lives. Stated briefly, the concept is that, unless the consideration involves something that provides food, shelter, financial resources to be used to acquire these (and other) necessities, the safety and security of themselves or their family members and friends; then it really isn't important in the long term for their happiness. Further, if it is possible to take a week to consider the relevance of what is being considered, do so. (It is preferred to making a knee-jerk decision that may prove to be a real mistake in the future). If it will not be important in the future- in say, 5 years or so, just forget about it. It does not seem necessary to spend effort, time, and resources to pursue it ultimately. Finally, at the end of the day when it is just you and your Creator, enjoy your night's rest after time spent in personal communications with him. Don't anticipate the troubles of another day (do not dwell on yesterday or worry about things well into the future). With all of these necessary aspects to living being accounted for while not being pressured by things that don't directly relate to these primary aspects of living; life will be much more carefree and less stressful. Fundamentally, this is at the core concerns for our existence; fuel for the body, availability of shelter and safety, having our immediate needs met, and having a good relationship with our source. Beyond this, it is debatable as to the relevance of the extraneous fluff that many people within secular society considers vital.

Things begin to get less than consensual when other aspects of society are considered as to their importance for specie continuance. Entertainment has a prominent place in western society as well as in many developing countries. Soccer, just to name one object of interest, is revered in many nations. The name of Hollywood takes on a place well beyond the place name for a city; instead it is a source of entertainment which continues a tradition that finds its roots in Broadway and, much earlier, to the cradle of civilization of ancient Greece. The arts, sports, music, drama, plays, and other forms of entertainment cultivate the spirit of inquiry and creativity. However, it is not at all clear to this author whether our Creator was concerned about this as a necessary commodity of importance to functioning. In fact, it is entirely reasonable to wonder if too many, if not most, people place more importance on entertainment than in leading a spiritual life. This is problematic to our long term interest. When it becomes more fashionable to go to a Sunday doubleheader of baseball rather than spend time in communion with the Creator, it appears relevant to this writer to conclude that the person has lost sight of what actually is important. Participations as a distraction to avoid facing life represents to me an immature, irresponsible approach to life that places our relationship with God as secondary to a primary interest in humanity.

All of this line of discussion leads to the question of "Is recreation and entertainment acceptable within a spiritual existence?" Yes, No, and It Depends are the three answers that I will forward. Recreation that allows the body to function at a high level and achieve its full development (using what the Creator has blessed us with) is acceptable. It really is a byproduct of individual involvement in the activity and having fun while sharing of themselves with others. It is not appropriate to me to spending money to be entertained by others who are paid obscene amounts of money because of the use of God-given talent. When I was a lad the athletes of my day played the game for the love of the sport rather than being primarily motivated for money. It seems senseless to idolize those whose talents are meager when compared to the Creator. He alone should be the object of idolizing as the one who has made everything possible in the universe.

The entertainment that allows our minds to focus on our relationship with each other, our natural environment, and our Creator is beneficial since it improves our sense of connectedness to the environment. Due to a better understanding of all that makes up the world of our existence from the by-products of entertainment; there is reasonably acceptable value when it is weighed based upon how it develops our relationship with the Creator positively. It is important to consider whether the importance the individual places on themselves as a child of the most High (or do they see God as merely one of many distractions within the existence of their daily life). When God doesn't occupy first place in the psyche of the person, then the entertainment that people engage in during the finite, un-renewable moments of their lives absent God while idolizing the created (celebrities and athletes, et. el.), is inappropriate. Further, it may often be detrimental to development of a spiritual relationship and is therefore not of relative equal importance to the relationship that ensures our immortal existence.

Everything that we perform, as a human being, should be directed to improving, stabilizing, or promoting a spiritual relationship with our Creator. In saying this it is worthy to state that this is the supreme purpose of our being. Regarding the relative importance of instant gratification versus delayed gratification is central to a determination as to whether the person is able to fully fulfill this ideal of spiritual connectedness. Impatience is a thorn in many individuals side as it robs the person of the ability to plan for the future and await its arrival. We want what we want, when we want it, and that does not mean waiting. When we do this we are short changing the person of experiencing the spiritual principles of seed time and harvest. One only need look at the planting process that includes the time from the inception of the seed into the ground, followed by germination, growth, and then bearing fruit to know that things follow a predictable strategy as prescribed by the Creator. We should not unrealistically see ourselves as being immune to this principle of nature as a creation of God. Even our existence is tied to this principle as coming from seed as well. And, we must understand that we will reap all that we sow in due time.

Besides the physical state of the organism, the mental state and mood of the organism is worthy of inquiry. It is directly related as important to our spiritual existence. We may either be neutral in our mood, positive in our mood, or distressed and/or negative in our mood. I can state, with a clear mind, that the Creator does not want his creation to be miserable or despondent. He would prefer for us to enjoy the benefits of a clear mind that is well and positively disposed. The absence of a spiritual relationship is at the foundation of the potential for much misery. We were meant to participate mentally and emotionally in a spiritual existence and the absence of that relationship is the seed for much illness. It represents the essence of effective coping with life as there is hope and a future after we are done here. This is beyond understanding for many today. But let it be clearly understood, God does not endeavor to engage with his creation as to what decisions he will make. We are intellectually but infants in comparison to his intellect. In short, God has not asked for our opinion, he is expecting our compliance and like with any parent/child relationship; there are ramifications for non-compliance. In short, our opinions are not important, our obedience is. We were endowed with free will to choose to engage in a relationship or not, failure to do so is not without a cost. However, due to the developed lack of reasonable fear of our Creator, we have placed our self on course to destroy the sum total of civilization due to our demonstrated ambivalence to entering into this relationship.

Along with a physically-sound and mentally/emotionally sound state of functioning is the question of faith as the foundational component to having a spiritual existence. I have heard the over-reported and useless statistic that says that upwards of 90% or more Americans believe in God. This is suggested as somehow being proof that the United States is a spiritual nation. It is also true that the coinage has the inscription of

"In God We Trust". However, it is also true that even the Devil and the demons believe that there is a God- they just don't obligate themselves to follow his lead. So it is only of a secondary importance that one says that they believe. Proof of belief involves the operation, in actions and deeds, of his expectations in order to have led a truly spiritual existence. Faith can be defined as knowing that things are going to be as the Creator plans them to play out. Things will be fine and beneficial however they play out with the best interests (and long term results) improving and complementing the spiritual life of the believer. Their faith bodes well for them based upon their belief in the one who will take them throughout the journey of living. He deserves all credit and glory for the outcome-it was not of our doing. After all, without him it is not guaranteed that we would even be afforded a single breath.

Perhaps a central consideration to attaining a sound emotional state is the ongoing development of a relationship with a mate with which to procreate for the continuation of the species. It is fundamental to the continued existence of the human race to accomplish the responsibility and joy of recreating in order to go forth and multiply. If we were to engage in relationships as being central to our emotional development without the inclusive of procreation, then the reported scriptural explanation to be fruitful and multiply would not have been stated. It fundamentally figured into the explanation for the genesis of the specie as an initially recorded pronouncement by our Creator. Is it important that the act of having a personal knowledge and experience of intimate, emotional expression-as well as the labeling of that emotion (love), be part of the catalog of human life events? On one level, it appears to be an experience that equips one to better be able to understand the concept of love thus it is invaluable to our development in that regard in our quest to be led by the concept. Considering that God is love, it is fundamentally necessary to understand the concept to appreciate his essence. In some cultures such as the Greek culture, love has many different words to describe it and it takes on many different forms such as a love for parent, friend, or partner. On the other hand, love without the ability to procreate is not in line with spiritual based, centuries-old, supported ideation. In fact, this writer has not observed the documentation within any spiritual traditions of a non-procreating relationship to be appropriate. Equally, within scriptures there are adverse documentations for non-potential procreation relationship as being negatively addressed in text associated to the Creator.

When I look at this presentation of the components for leading a spiritual life and, the brief mention thus far of negligible aspects of living, I must admit that there is many more obvious, insignificant aspects to the daily circus called life. They include the extensive range from what politicians and celebrities say and do. It appears to me that the media covers these items in order to fill their programming needs due to the absence of important and timely issues to present. After all, who cares if the President plays golf; he may or may not have stunk up the greens. My question is related to whether it does anything productive to cure our ills as a nation and promote our responsibilities as a positive contributor for the betterment of others in the world. (It does not provide food, cloth, heal, or insure the best interests of anyone and serves as to fill a time slot to take up unused air time for the media outlet).

Why do I care what a teenager or early adult entertainer says or thinks? Their full cognitive capacity (dependent on their chronological, developmental age) may not even be fully achieved. In reality, they do not appear to be authorities on much of anything (they are acknowledged for singing a song, not trying to tell any responsible adult how to live). It also appears relative to acknowledge that these individuals sometimes self-destruct while receiving undeserved, unwarranted attentions for debauchery and, sometimes, criminal mischief. Does anyone really care where a personality vacationed, visited, or spent time engaged in during the activity of daily living? Finally, how does a person who has limited education get into a situation on television where they are allowed to have air time to verbalize their theory on life? This is usually not supported by the benefit of any actuarially supported research and education while trying to tell others right from wrong. Do they think that they have insight which is particularly significant beyond the opinions of another person? I believe it is equally imperative to know the training that celebrities have that equips them with the expertise to merit passing on to the general public their views and attitudes? I venture to consider that they really don't have more going on cognitively than many others of the populace. So, why should I care about their opinions or seriously consider their, frequently liberal, expressions? In all of these instances, and many more, it does not really matter. However, I would be inappropriate if I did not acknowledge that many personalities do great charity work. For those efforts they should be appreciated immensely.

Many people go beyond the mere accumulation of the needs list acknowledged thus far and are predisposed to consume and to acquire things. A common bumper sticker displayed in present-day society suggests that those who died with the most things, somehow "won". It is uncertain to me how the acquisition of many items unrelated to the direct continuity of the human race (or ensuring a beneficial immortality) is vital and inherently useful. First, one must have bigger and bigger places to store these things. Then, they must have security measures and the need for a police force to ensure that they don't get stolen (and the owner injured in the theft of these items). They then acquire still more related things in order to make their collections complete. As is obvious, this tendency is not particularly useful and expedient to being able to function at a relaxed rate absent stress, with the end result being that the materials take up more important a place than the relationship with a Creator. As such, it is realistic to consider that the acquisition of goods is unimportant when they do not relate directly to the functioning of the creation. Further, if they don't assist in growing our relationship with the Creator, their importance doesn't seem obvious to me.

Not only is the use of resources of significance, the utilization of time is also profound for our development of a spiritual existence. A good indicator of the effectiveness of a person towards ensuring the perpetuity of the species can be found in how their time was utilized. Likewise, the use of time is our signature on our value for what our Creator has given us. Did we use the resources that were rendered to our care in a manner that brings a smile to the Creator's lips and joy to his being? In an earlier time of history entire cities spent the lifetimes of many generations of inhabitants to erect churches to the glory of the Creator. These structures serve as a symbol of the connectedness of the inhabitants to their God. I am hard pressed to find the same dedication in the present-day within the western world. Now, it is more often common to see time spent in the acquisition of wealth and possessions (not to mention position and receipt of preferential treatment). So, it is relative to forward the argument that the present use of time is ill-spent. It is not directed to the development of a personal relationship with our Creator; thereby qualifying as being of dubious value.

In the presentation thus far prescribed it bears noting, not considered is the fact that a significant number of people do attend to important functions such as raising their children. (However, statistics vary as to just how little actual time is spent in direct conversation with our off springs daily). Work is accomplished in order to acquire the resources to pay for our needs and responsibilities. (Here again, close to half of the U.S. population is in receipt of some form of financial support from the government treasury bureau that is received without direct work- related activities). And, a few individuals spend time attending church and involving themselves in a communal relationship with their Creator. The key word here is "a few" as the statistics are not comforting regarding attendance.

It appears that many Americans are intoxicated (if not literally, then figuratively) by their own world status. Some ignore the responsibility to contribute to the continuation of the species, nationally or internationally. We do demonstrate some concern for others without regard for what part of the world where people suffer (we are a charitable lot). However, we provide many of these financial resources to places that wish us ill and despise our principles. What is unclear and conspicuously absent is the present lack of identification with the values and traditions that have brought us to this position of preeminence in the world. I can't fathom how the present time frame of the past 50 years can realistically assume that they have more wisdom than the previous 6 thousand years of recorded history.

A common thread to the present humanistic movement is that man is god, and God is irrelevant. This is what I have observed to be the demonstrated humanistic behavior in both principle and practice fundamentally. All of those stalwarts of civilization as they relate to family and faith lie wasted on the scrapheap of the present age. Our heritage that has been based on our world's accomplishments are debated, denied, or ignored. It truly doesn't seem to matter to the secular present-day human that its means of continuance and connectedness to its source is being lost. This appears to be due to immediate need considerations that deny the obligation to be led by fundamentally sound principles associated with life. (I have actually been told by clients that their "god" is their children or a door; totally baffling to someone who acknowledges the omnipotent nature of a Creator and his Son).

Communication is a key to the cooperation and cohabitation of the human race and is thereby essential to the peaceful coexistence of the species. (Not to mention its contribution for the ability for us to live as a unit and accomplish progress in the human's survival). Within the past 20 years a disturbing trend has occurred with the advent of a society that is bent on individual isolation. Concerning our work life, some are now being able to work from home (thereby avoiding interactions). The youth and early adults within the country now have what is called social media for their preferred means of communication. This form consists of communicating over a computer rather than in person. Many multi-million (and perhaps billon) dollar business deals are consummated over a computer screen or by video conferencing. Further, governments discuss the security and safety of the world's population indirectly also. The point is that, by traditional estimates that I first learned in an introductory military educational class, approximately 90% of communication is found to be non-verbal. Primarily, it consists of body language, facial expressions, and the syntax, style of verbal diction, and accent to the spoken word. All of this is primarily non-existent due to the lack of personal, face-to-face touch communication patterns that are being discarded. There is nothing inherently social about social media; it obviously doesn't appear to matter if one is concerned about getting a real feel for and understanding of others.

A continuity of the species is a topic that is seldom addressed and very incompletely understood but, nevertheless, of great value in an understanding of the future integrity to the human race. It is necessary in regards to considering the potential for our world's continued existence. Within the past 90 years the United States has become an urban society while moving away from the country. In large part, the advent of communication advances and efficient means of transportation (namely the car) has supported this occurrence. As of the 1920s and 1930s, the average family had lived in the same location for multiple generations. The multi-generational interactions of grandparents, parents, children, and other relatives were at the forefront of their social life (predominately in the rural areas). This was evidenced by multiple extended family groups living in the same general neighborhoods. The responsibility of ensuring the smooth transfer of knowledge to the younger generations was attended to by the grandparents who taught to their children who then, in turn, instructed the children in the ways that would lead to their appropriate growth and maturity. They learned the lessons that related to being safe as a human being, to being self sufficient, and procreating the species.

They developed physically, emotionally, and spiritually and were given instruction into the importance of the precepts of civilizations and of the need to continue the values and traditions of their forefathers. Soon thereafter, (especially at the conclusion of World War II) the younger generations began moving away across the country in search of employment and in search of financial gain and opportunity. Soon thereafter, the mother became the additional breadwinner as the family unit became more obsessed with the accumulation of property. This trend was in address to societies' insistence of having more which occurred at the expense of a more close-knit, interrelated family unit. This new reality meant that there is frequently no parent to watch the children after school often times. This led to a lack of assurance that school work was accomplished and that the child stayed out of harm's way (and out of mischief).

This change in family dynamics has led to the development of gangs where the child can find attachment to replace that which is now lacking. Due to the pursuit of property, the family gained a possessions advantage at the expense of interrelatedness. The essence of the definition of, and function of, the family were terminally rendered harmed and has led to a lack of sanctity of the family as being responsible for all that it had one time been associated with. Now, children are part of a strategy and are "planned" with the inconvenience of childbirth being remedied by termination which is considered to be a "right". In short, we have become less interested in family and more interested in the advantages of property and convenience at the expense of the continuity of the family unit. In fact, we now propose the addition of non-reproductive units to become accepted as "family".

And, to account for this lack of attention to the continuity of the species by traditional means, we expect and allow for strangers to have the responsibility for raising our children (school systems) and have relinquished our rights to engage in non-prescribed disciplinary functions to address unacceptable juvenile behavior. Although some excessive uses of corporal punishment have made it necessary to address obvious childhood abuse, it is not feasible to entertain using many forms of discipline for their own children due to the potential intrusions of the legal system into their life. This is the anticipated response to be gained for their efforts at raising a responsible and societal compliant citizen, or, so it is assumed by many parents that have been congenial enough to express such misgivings. Again, does it matter that we are becoming less able to continue the orderly progression of the species into succeeding generations. This results when tradition and respect are not addressed with the support of available discipline, when indicated?

However, there is the idea of family from another more theoretical stance that includes the total sum of humankind as a single entity that is reliant on the individual structures known as the organism (the human). The simple fact is that not all of the species are self-sustaining. There are some human members who are reliant upon the benevolence of others for their livelihood and survival. On the circumstance of individual age of the species it is apparent that those very young and those whom are very old are dependent for their survival on that assistance. Further, the organisms which are defective in a manner that precludes their ability to operate fully on par with their peer's leads to the need for help.

It is of one of the highest spiritual principles that we place ourselves last and have a basis otherness or selflessness that has the best interests of others ahead of us. If we don't, we are merely selfish and self-serving or so it seems appropriate to consider. It is this sense of humanity that makes us vulnerable as an organism but, paradoxically, affords us our greatest strength. This situation requires a common ground and common interest which may be less than relevant to the present condition. Only when an emergency that threatens the mutual stability of all occurs do we refocus our attention and energies to the benefit of our fellow human being. It is this incident of otherness, which is a true indicator of our spiritual nature in actuality. In the present instance it appears that this may not matter as narcissistic, me-first tendencies have become prevalent.

The real factor that assaults these well intentioned attitudes for existences of otherness and selflessness is an adverse attitude prevalent at the present era for right of entitlement. As a young child growing up, the act of receiving aid from others, government included, was a source of embarrassment. One only relied on this aid in the absolute, most dire circumstances. No one wanted to be the subject of conversation by their neighbors regarding being on the government "dole". The principle of self-reliance was etched in stone. Everyone was proud of their own efforts at attaining whatever station that they were able to secure. One did not have a desire to have whatever was on the market. With the advent of effective advertising, an obsession with the possession of things made whatever means that was available to securing those things became acceptable. What was once a source of embarrassment is now the consistent choice of many who do not believe that they alone are responsible for the supplying their wants or needs. Instead, they believe that public welfare is the vehicle for having their wants taken care of, and not only just the satisfaction of their basic needs.

Now individual believe that the government owes me because there is a program for that purpose. I must have my fair share appears to be the idea. What has occurred in reality is that nowadays people have lost touch with the reality that the government is made up of your community, neighbors, state, and fellow citizens living in the United States. They are the ones who are providing the funds to the government by the sweat from their brow when engaging in the activity of work. When one gets money from the government they are actually getting money from their neighbor's work efforts. This is the actual reality that they have conveniently avoiding recognizing so as not to be forced to entertain that they are being financed by their neighbor. The only difference is that the individual does not have to forego the embarrassment of walking next door to ask directly for money from their neighbor. In effect, the government is playing what amounts to a shell game.

Within this discourse the family, the human considerations, the continuity and development of humans, and modern-day assaults on the time honored and valued practices and procedures has been transiently addressed. So the question is that, if there are so many things that aren't important," How does one determine what is important?" The easiest answer is that there are some very fundamental questions that hold the key to a determination as to what matters. What promotes the development of the human race in compliance with our Creator, while not rendering us obsolete, is an ongoing concern. Also, addressing the danger of fundamental vulnerability to extinction due to stupidity is of primary importance.

Once it is determined that the organism can survive, then, how can it thrive? A central feature of this book is to forward the principle that, without God within the life of the individual and a subsequent spiritual connection, it cannot thrive. And, also, what allows a person to thrive while not being intrusive or detrimental to other people is to be desired. Any human that is taken out of the context of that of which it was intended will mutate. It is feasible to address whether the recent past, present, and near future incursions onto those functional standards that have been in force for the past 6 thousand years will lead to a fundamental, irreversible damage. As an individual that believes in the infinite tolerance of a Creator that wants what is best for his creation and of the inherent tendency for the creation to inadvertently end each test by leaning towards organism integrity provides hope. We will have some who will not fail their Creator. I believe that this hope may go unrealized as there is a potential grave danger that our future may not continue based upon our present race towards self-imposed extinction.

I am sure that many who have invested the time and energy to read thus far have a common thought that they do not believe, as my writing has suggested, we are really that close to an end. We have had problems in the past and we have managed to gets things straightened out so, why is now any different? (Kind of like the rubber ducky in the tub of water that always resurfaced when the child takes his hand off of it underwater-it always bobs up to the surface). What has changed is that the spiritual foundation (previously present) is now lacking whereas before it had some extensive existence within the population as a whole. This foundation allowed for the basis of what became described as a revival and, in essence, was a return to our spiritual roots (throughout time we have had these movements which are historically recorded). Since I feel that the foundation is not available, thus the reason for my dim suggestions.

Further, an earlier psychologist who provided important research which has served as a model for our basis of understanding about moral development (Kohlberg) suggested that at the greatest level of refinement and best example of total moral development, one considers the world as to what will be the need that is universally applicable when it might not be personally beneficial or popular with those who are in charge and able to make one's life miserable. Being led with the interest of the world and, in my instance, of regarding my Creator and his Son as the basis for my existence, I press on and face those who feel insulted or disturbed by my provided insight to promote a return to our source. I fear sincerely that we are within a flash of seeing our world dissolve literally. As such, I am sharing my concerns and fears for our possible dissolution.

One of the main events that supported the beginning of emphasis on science (and practical basis for my fear) was in the experiencing of the use of the atomic bomb at the end of World War II. For the first time in our history people realized that they-humans, could completely finish themselves off in totality. The entire history of our civilization, from the earliest known records to the present, demonstrates an ongoing advancement of the means of killing each other as a guiding accomplishment for each global power. At present, we often do not demonstrate sufficient cognitive capital (or the use of it) to secure that this potential will go unrealized. Even more real, there are those who see their own death and destruction as acceptable as long as they destroy everyone else who does not share their personal religious faith. Their faith also is based upon the belief that this destruction, that they claim is for their God, will lead to a purely hedonistic opportunity for physical, sexual experiences. This is in comparison to the theorized basis for our Christian heritage of love, charity, and hope. Does it not seem that by present secular standards, based upon their responses toward us, Christians are the enemy of society instead?

My fundamental belief is that most present-day world inhabitants are primarily interested in realizing their needs being met while living with their proverbial heads in the sand. As an old time expression captures the situation, and what is clear to me, "and the band played on", essentially captures the picture of how it may invariably end. Evidence of this expressed belief is that, as humans, we don't even personally realize the extent of the destruction of this invention called the atomic bomb. The sheer extent of the desolation from the use of science, absence of any surviving plant, animal, or human life after its use, is not even understood. Those who would choose to bring it to bear on those they are in dispute with don't clearly demonstrate having this insight. This lack of a deep, meaningful awareness of the individual stories of misery and obscene termination of hope for those affected by the detonation is but further evidence of what serves as the basis for my fears. The full understanding of the unbearable loss is unimaginable to our fragile, yet simple, approach to our world. The flesh and blood entity that is expected to be compliant to their God must be the focus of our concerns, not the pursuit of treasure and pleasure to fulfill our needs being met, absent others. God's law is central to our existence, not man being preoccupied with themselves throughout their days as is the current way many live.

What is of further consideration is how we can go about the completion of the design that we were formed within and being compliant to the wishes of that one who has formed us. I see the analogy of the moth as fitting to describe the state of humankind within the context of the present age. The moth flies closer and closer to the light in spite of the fact that the heat generated from the light will kill it if it proceeds too closely to the light. In spite of this danger, the moth flutters towards and away from the light with the only perceivable pattern being that the moth invariable gets closer as time continues. Finally, after some maneuvering and starting and stopping, the moth makes contact with the light. The light does not immediately exterminate the moth but renders it flawed and terminally affected. Within a fairly short time, the moth makes a final dive towards the light and then falls away, spent and deceased. There is continued evidence that any species, faced with removal from its origins, will lose its way and venture too close to that which can extinguish it. In essence, we continue to perform this dance without any realistic attention to the facts that we are within a mistake of extermination. It is something to consider.

Chapter Four

The Reality of the Haves and the Have Not's

Recently a coworker informed me that he had heard on a news broadcast that, in over 14 states in the United States, individuals who depended on public assistance actually had access to more disposable income than many of those who worked for close to, or at, minimum wage. In another instance, a newscasters on cable news stations state that an individual can gain the equivalent of upwards of over $40 thousand dollars, or more, yearly in things called "free stuff" from the government. These things included such as child care, food stamps, rental assistance or outright payments, medical and mental health care and insurance coverage, college and technical school free tuition, and assistance with utilities payments or reductions in utility rates due to limited income. A further statement that I had originally heard over 40 years ago (and too numerous times to mention since then) that is certainly true for a sizeable portion of Americans with little employable skills is, "Why work, I can make more money if I stay at home and just sit on my couch and watch television?"

Where is the incentive to go out and expend sweat equity if you can see others walk the streets casually socializing while you are working to pay your bills? In comparison, does it seem fair to engage in work as compared to others enjoying luxuries that you cannot afford from working? You do what seems to be the responsible thing while they may be placing out their hand for a subsidy rather than engage in the activity of work? It really is not surprising that the number of people who depend on the government for assistance continues to swell to figures approaching over 50% of the United States population. Close to half of the population is in receipt of some form of government spending programs. Although a portion of that number of individuals have earned what they are receiving (Social Security retirement, unemployment insurance, et. el.) there is still a statistically significant number of people who have developed the mindset that government's role is to provide for them. This is absent any individual initiative to be self-sufficient. It bears repeating that their working neighbors who pay taxes, as well as the foreign governments lending money to America in order to buy it outright, are subsidizing these individual's income. This is not about those who continually pay into benefit programs and justly draw out during temporal periods of personal misfortune. Instead, this is about the many that prefer spending program benefits to self-provision from employment. This is not a suggestion that those who routinely pay into the government should not be allowed to rely on financial resources during old age or during illness or loss of jobs, only that those who can work should do so.

This paradox has another element that cannot be ignored or glossed over. Those who are receiving the aide are in possession of things and services that a significant portion of the world population may not have even conceived of. They do not possess these items for them self. Television, running water and toilets, heat or cool dependent on the season, cell phones, cable television service, internet and computer ownership/use, and a pantry of food items that exceeds that which is necessitated to surpass the limited nutritional resources of a sizeable portion of the world population represents a short list of the items in discussion. Other people in less developed areas of the world may go to bed hungry at night. In our society we consider our citizens, who have all of these aspects to their living arrangement present, but who have less than a base amount of financial income to spend on goods, as living at the poverty level. It sounds harsh to point this out as we, as a society, take for granted these amenities and believe that they are just essential and therefore not to be considered as a luxury. Fact is, in many areas or the world they are luxuries. We need to face the harsh reality that we live beyond our means as a nation when we think that all of our citizens "need" to have a monetary stipend from the government. The unmet need of financial resources leads to seeking employment-the satisfaction of their needs (absent work) leads to an entitled mentality without personal effort to achieve self-sufficiency.

This does not mean that there are not many who do have a need for assistance; the question of what is enough and when is the assistance enough is the question being asked. If someone is receiving money to spend and all of the additional assistance that has been discussed is also present, then we have to decide better as to what assistance is enough. Further, when is it too much in comparison to those who choose to work instead to support the needs of them self and their family? It seems to me that someone working should have more resources than those who do not, otherwise, why bother?

The actual issue is the conflict between two principles that have been a part of our culture since our early days. On the one hand, when one works hard and applies themselves-they stand to gain and succeed and, on the other hand, those who have should be prepared to provide for the less fortunate. The existing problem is that liberalism sees any success as qualification to provide for others. Often, the result of today's application of these ideals is a loss for the ones who struggle to succeed by working. There are no qualifying criteria other than for the person to claim that they "can't" make it so the government needs to help them. In some cases, "can't" is substituted for it is "difficult to get by and get more than the bare minimum" so the government is expected to assist the individual. This help is in achieving the accumulation of those thing on their "want" list rather than their "need" list. It has become easier to accept a handout than to apply oneself to the activity of work is the suggestion that is implied by this behavioral mindset. It bears noting that it is certainly not a problem to receive temporary service in order to better work-related skills and receive training to be productive in the workforce. Nor should it be improper to receive assistance when ill and disabled. It is the terminal recipients of benefits when this is not clearly the case to which I speak of. This is absent any effort or desire to be personally reliant.

A cultural issue has been at work to a significant degree within this discussion as well. There exists a well-demonstrated process that reinforced the idea that government is responsible for the interests of various groups based upon historical wrongs. This is evidenced by ongoing programs, laws, and policies to address needs of the disenfranchised. The idea has taken hold, within some cultural entities, that government will come through therefore it is not imperative to depend upon personal initiative in order to survive. It would not be appropriate to blame any ethnic or cultural group for this mindset. It is the liberal policies of our government of the past 50 years that have cultivated this lack of self-reliance. This dependent mindset has replaced the "can do" spirit that was previously the moniker of the average American. Prior to this time people found satisfaction in their own efforts and pride in their accomplishments. This new way of thinking that depends on government largess is insidious to the lifeblood of the republic and non-spiritual. It deems the concept of using the talents and abilities provided by our Creator to the individual, to honor God by their wise use, to be irrelevant. Present political mindset is that any group of peoples who have been treated poorly or, outright immorally, in the past are now entitled to be given preferred privilege as a means of leveling the playing field. This is considered just since they are, according to the government, "disenfranchised". This does not appear to make logical sense to me, as those who were mistreated, should have been honored by dealing with transgressors when they mistreated others. Instead, the government says that their descendants are to be considered preferentially based upon past wrongs. This is instead of treating all people fairly and living out the creed based on the content of character instead of providing preference to anyone over another. When we lose our pride in ourselves as a people honored by our Creator, while not holding all in equal esteem, (and responsible for being productive as a testimony to him), we have dishonored him. We risk being held in contempt.

Scripturally, it is stated that he who does not work should not eat. This was the litmus test in the days of the Jamestown colony when survival of the colonist was not assured. In our past immigrant heritage, one worked to survive and did not benefit from government financial support but not today. Those who have, in many instances, done little to contribute to the social fabric of the country are afforded such a mind numbing assortment of benefits that the average American cannot begin to fathom the reasoning that allows for such excess. Further, many are barred from receiving in-kind support. For a significant portion of our history we were justifiably proud of the efforts of the citizens to improve the standard of living for all. When we arrived into the 20th century, with inventions that have made life at ease, we have become allowed to have leisure activities to a degree unlike previously experienced in our past. Entertainment is now a significant part of our life. Before electricity and heating/cooling units inception, the free time during the spring, summer, and fall was spent collecting firewood for the winter in order to avoid freezing during the chills of winter. Lack of industrialization and assembly line processes meant that considerable time was spent tailoring clothes by the female members of the family. The male counterparts of the house were responsible for cultivating a plot of land with vegetables for canning of food and a fall slaughter of fattened stock for the winter (as well as feeding the brood during the summer months from the garden).

Times have changed and our load has dramatically been eased due to those many inventions. However, our mindset has also. Now everyone is supposed to have without any consideration for individual toil and effort previously exerted. This plays out when the number of, in excess of, 18 trillion dollars in U.S. government public debt is acknowledged. This is what the United States government owes at this point supposedly with others calculating additional actual debt that is not clearly understood. Our luxury has led to a state where-in essence, every man, woman, and child individually has a potential responsibility for a bill of in excess of $50 thousand each.

Essentially, the field of entertainment has developed as an offshoot of our hedonistic self-interest that has mushroomed due to available time previously unavailable because of the lack of inventions and the resultant convenience. Further, this ease in our burden associated with living has had an indirect impact on society. A decreased understanding of the value of money due to decreased effort being expended (as a result of the inherent luxury afforded us from technology) ends up being a factor in the lack of frugality of individual and governmental management of financial resources. (We don't experience the full extent of toil to accomplish things as we previously did due to the conveniences gained from our technological revolution). Our desire to meet the needs of everyone, and allow all to enjoy the leisure that has come from the availability of technology, has led to a lack of the practice of common sense and borders insanity. In the process, the survival instincts of the populace have essentially evaporated and most would be hard pressed to demonstrate the abilities and skills needed to survive if things degenerate as they appear to be heading. This conclusion is arrived at when one considers the austere state concerning food and water supplies, weather condition trends, and disharmony between the ethnic and religious subsections on the planet.

How is this rambling spiritual? God gave many of us the ability to fend for ourselves as long as we exercised a substantive amount of effort to meet our needs. When we fail to utilize the skills, ingenuity, and physical ability to fulfill our responsibility to ourselves then we are not honoring God's efforts to provide us the wear-with-all to subsist. And I do mean subsist. It is not always about having leisure and excess. Sometimes we should find satisfaction and gratitude in having enough. That is what is spiritual about this abject larceny of taking from those who strive to achieve in order to subsidize those who fail to make efforts to succeed. As I have already stated, there are some who need help. We should not belittle others for their plight; however a system must be devised to separate the wheat from the chaff. In the 1990's the idea was reflected in the law that those receiving government assistance must work at something that was beneficial to society. It has degenerated to the point that now going to a class or reading a book has been suggested as being sufficient to account for government handouts. What is next?

It seems very non-spiritual for the individual to ask the Creator for any benefit or assistance when the individual is not presently using the abilities that have already been given to them to address their wishes. If one is trying to the best of one's ability, then it is appropriate to anticipate that God will help. After all-would any of us not assist our children when they have put out an honest effort and are deserving of assistance? God is no different, and he rewards those who strive to achieve. The problem is now that many others expect to profit from another individual's striving for achievement. This is due to abuses in taxing those who work, thus carrying on their collective backs the individuals who prefer government support. And, the excesses of government taxation that provide, in effect, government-determined charity practices, have led to no conscious, personal understanding of being charitable for the needs of their neighbors.

In an earlier time when charity was given from their own available provisions that were grown and harvested by the provider the act of giving was clear in both giving and receiving. (Now, people don't actually see the impact of their charity in the lives of others or even know who is getting their tax revenues). In the early days of the nation, there were no influential church groups, not-for-profit organizations to provide support, or activist associations to step in and the generosity of your neighbor may be the only thing that allowed you to survive when you experienced tragedy. Now, the existence of food suppliers, lack of individual participation in the direct collection of supplies for subsistence, and availability of the government to supply financial and other resources has brought us to a place where some do not even appreciate in an insightful way, the ideas associated with charity, either in the receipt of it or in the offering of oneself to benefit less fortunate.

This does not mean that charity does not continue to be practices at the present time. Instead, charity provides substantive support while allowing some who manage it to live in sometimes reported splendor. The empathic, personal sensitivity associated with the act of giving may not be realized. Thus, the full effect of this Judeo-Christian growth experience of helping others is not active in some instances. This is due to being forced to participate by taxation-rather than having a reality check which equips us with a personal feeling of compassion for others in society in those times when we lend a hand.

So it ends up that, at present, those who have, in reality, do not have. At least not in comparison with what they have worked for is many cases. What they have worked for is dived up for those who don't have. Therefore those who, theoretically, do not have, really do have and it is the result of the work of others who they don't even know. On top of this, some are being told that they are not providing their "fair share" because they are *only* supplying 25 to 40% of what they earn to support others. Frequently, their support is for those who have determined that staying out of the work force is more desirable than engaging in the industry of work. (In some cases over 60% of the income of wealthy, successful people is taken in the form of the various taxes to include federal, state, local, and municipality). At the present time, less than 50% of Americans are financially providing the tax base that provides for a figure approaching 50% of Americans who are not paying into the tax base of the government. Often, these people see tax time as an opportunity to have an extra check to spend. It is appropriate to believe that the sheer madness associated with this will continue as it relates to the dynamics of the U.S. voting habits. It seems reasonable to believe that the more than 50% who are receiving government financial support would be expected to continue voting for the candidates who ensure that they continue to have their financial needs met. This results in the scenario of the less than 50% who pay for the entitlement programs being outvoted at the ballot box. In practical reality, this results in a position of economic slavery for those who contribute to the tax base supporting the majority electorate who are provided monies from the minority voting block that gives the tax revenues for the U.S. Treasury. This plays out by ending up to be the basis for provide free stuff (financial support) from the government.

To make my point, observe the one who is unemployed and collecting financial support. I have seen instance when one reaches the end of their time frame for collection of benefits and then magically finds something to do to earn a living. If it was possible to find the position at the conclusion of the collection of the benefits then why was it not possible to do so when one had been collecting benefits earlier? Go figure. Or I could reflect on the time that I saw a person who spent the day panhandling on a busy intersection. At approximately 5PM he walked down the street to the nearby gas station and got in a Cadillac and drove off. When one sees such excessive arrogance it leaves one with the attitude of anger and resentment. This results in the few making it hard to empathize with those who do need our help and concern. These are the things that cause one to become less than totally enamored with our benefit system. Not to mention how it makes it harder for the deserving ones who need help and support when there is such fraud, abuse, and irresponsibility.

There is a vital understanding that must be crossed in the discernment of this chapter and of the points that are included in the text. Every individual on the planet is absolutely precious and of unfathomable value to the Creator. He does not want any of us to go without our needs (not wants) being met if appropriate. This principle is not lost on a liberal-minded electorate that attempts to support the various governmental programs that are made to address these needs with the utility of that argument. What is not party to the discussion is, "Are we really acting in the best interest of people when we allow for handouts to take the place of gainful employment?" And let me be further clear in using personal experience to reinforce who is able to benefit from the activity of work and, who is not. In a simple, basic manner I have seen where work allowed one to have a psychologically positive self-concept and this is a primary attribute to appreciate. Remember, not everyone is attempting to circumvent the system and some are truly in need of help and we, as lovers of people, are bound to help. The real challenge lies in acceptance that the number of those who are receiving assistance, realistically, is not tied to who are truly unable to provide for themselves through the activity of work.

A manager at a facility when I was employed at before my time suffered with polio. He came to work each day and moved around the work area in spite of his limitations. His movements were a struggle on more than one occasion but we were in awe of his spirit and motivation to go forward. He did not ask for or allow any help, sympathy, or special considerations and he earned a substantial sum as his payroll. He continues to work into his later post-employment era by painting pictures and I have been told his work is quite good in spite of only having one unaffected hand and arm. Further, this individual's successor was affected by cerebral palsy and worked for a significant term as a competent manager. She was a trusted associate to the department head for a large government agency. She could have easily have been awarded disability, as could the manager in the position before her, but they choose to work and flourish in spite of their circumstances. These are but two instances of what is a larger picture where those who have had to overcome obstacles have done so rather than succumb to the temptation to become reliant on the generosity of the government. I can go further.

A family member who provided an excellent example of behavior for my upbringing was afflicted with arthritis to the degree that he was unable to bend his legs, his feet were folded up onto themselves, and he had to shuffle on his toes with canes whenever he attempted to move. He had paid out of his own pocket (from a long term saving plan) for a house with cash. He purchased a car specially altered to be driven with arm operated levers so as not to need to use his legs and feet and rarely missed a day from work on an assembly line. He eventually retired to a pension after a career standing on his feet each day for a significant amount of time assembling vending machines. He did not ever, in the 50+ years that I knew him, complain about his condition and he made every effort to be self-sufficient. Further, he praised his Creator on a daily basis. He could have relied on disability, instead, he decided that he would persevere in spite of the hand he had been dealt. So, when someone tells me that I just don't understand I believe that it is just the opposite. I do understand that they can be a contributor, and after spending time overcome the problems associated with their situation unsuccessfully, should only then consider accepting assistance. Not just say, "I can't" or "It's difficult" and do them self a disservice by not allowing for the chance to grow or develop spiritually through the exercise of the mind, body, and spirit in the activity that God has provided for us called work.

Any person, like myself, who calls people to task for accepting government stipends in lieu of work are called "haters" by the liberal-minded media and mainstream America. (They really don't demonstrate the ability or logical reasoning skills to address anyone in any other fashion rather than to attach a label to those who disagree with them. It appears to show to me a base ignorance as well as I can tell and is reminiscent of what I saw in the early years of elementary school behaviorally). It bears noting that this use of label and expressed word represents, as best I can understand from reflection and guidance provided from an elderly spiritual family member, to be the result of the experienced emotional discomfort absent any higher-level rational reasoning exercises. It also supposes that they are unable or unwilling to recognize that they may be, in practice, immoral or manipulating for an undeserved advantage.

As Christ stated when he left his disciples, there would be a comforter sent to attend to us while we try to live on the planet. Various religions have different ways of explaining it (i.e. conscience) yet, for me, it is the Holy Spirit that lives in me with the spirit, in essence, convicting me when I personally know when I am wrong. It is the practice of avoidance of responsibly considering what the spirit within is trying to tell the person and, instead, lashing out at those who provide the substance which causes the reality of sin to be acknowledged personally. This seems to be preferred to looking inward and doing what is required to become compliant with the awareness from the spirit. There is a reality that seems to be lost on these individuals. They can't seem to fathom the simplicity to the situation.

Concerning the label of hater in the context of our fiscal irresponsibility we only need have a primary and simple means of assessing the situation. We have X amount of dollars coming into the U.S. Treasury in the form of taxes, tariffs, and fees. These revenues serve to provide for our necessities and, if anything is left over, we can invest in infrastructure or education to name but a few of the preferences that have been address by the government. This is much the same as the individual household in America. We must balance the income versus the outlays of bills, groceries, and needs of the family members. It you don't have the money to purchase it then you have to figure what can wait, what is needed right now, or do you need to work more to gain the additional funds needed to fulfill what is necessary. Unfortunately, the U.S. Government hasn't learned or practiced this lesson in the past 40+ years (for the most part). It is really that simple-however for the majority of liberal-minded individuals who call those who question their extravagant spending sprees as haters. Actually, it could not be any less complicated that quantum physics it seems by their lack of insight. And, when we experience bankruptcy as a nation-what will we call those who have pointed at us as haters for expecting financial austerity?

Chapter Five

Do We Have a Right to Ignore Others?

When If It Doesn't Affect Me-It Isn't My Business, Doesn't Work

In spite of the adage that "if it doesn't affect me, don't get involved", it really will ultimately have a direct or indirect effect on each of us. Although, indirectly, someone who is important to you such as a son, daughter, grandchild, or neighborhood acquaintance may suffer due to ambivalence to active societal involvement. I can't begin to number the amount of times I have heard someone utter that adage and then complain at a future date about the very thing that they chose to previously excuse or ignore. This attitude is central to how we got to where we are at present. The mindset is the exercise of an avoidance mechanism of humans that allows for immoral and unspiritual lifestyles to develop, grow, and flourish. Unless addressed, this avoidance will serve to contribute to our undoing. The dislike for confrontation forms the basis for the growth and existence of amoral behavior in our midst. This attitude is terminal for a number of reasons and affects us in multiple levels at the international, national, state, and local levels of living.

This adage leads to excessive criminal activity and amoral activities that we pay excessive sums of money to house those in penal institutions who we ignored initially. We have the loss of life of those we care about due to this lack of proactive action to address the suspect behaviors. We have lost our sense of community which is demonstrated by locking ourselves in our homes, avoid going out after dark, and arm ourselves with weapons to deal with those who might attempt to rob, injure, or kill us. Instead of meeting in the communities and getting to know the neighborhood, we often don't really know our neighbors. Later we read about someone who lives right down the street who has been charged with criminal activity. The suspect had lived right on our street for a prolonged period of time right in our midst. Much fun has been made of the nosey neighbor in television sitcoms in previous years to a point when it was considered rude to know much about those who share our residential area. This suggests that we fail to act to consider our survival wherein one needs to be aware of one's surroundings in order to ensure their security. And to further elaborate on the point, is it not getting rather frequent to see sheriff cars racing down the road through traffic with lights flashing and sirens blaring each day. In my early days this event was unusual and a topic of conversation. What is going on when we just consider this event an annoyance and the reality of today while continuing on without any concern?

On the state and national level the notion that those who are concerned about moral and spiritual issues are just trying to control others and are not allowing for individual freedom is the consensus.

We are told that there is truly no right and wrong, just "gray areas" and we must just try to accept others (or so we are instructed). Acceptance and tolerant are noble and worthy traits, yet, when we don't condone the behavior for our own off springs, why do we accept and legislate in favor of those behaviors for others? Practically addressed, is it not dysfunctional to have a separate code of conduct for our self than for others? It belies logic to think that one can be personally offended and nauseated by an immoral act but have that behavior or lifestyle allowed to be supported by legal sanction for our society.

It further confounds practical judgment when smoking pot, a known gateway drug, becomes legalized thereby expanding the number and types of intoxicants available for legal consumption. These substances feed the threat to life and property associated with driving offenses and crimes to secure resources to purchase and traffic them. It is still debatable as to whether it is permissible to allow someone to destroy themselves by abusing their bodies; on the other hand it is not open to conjecture to destroy those who are not directly involved. Only in our "civilized society" that babbles on about "individual freedom" is such permissible.

We would be wise to acknowledge that it is our business, even when we believe otherwise, and act accordingly. Everything that we say that doesn't affect us directly usually indirectly becomes a tax to our pocketbooks. Where do you think all of the money to supply the needs of immigrants who come here illegally, in base avoidance of our policies comes from? They gain the resources to sustain themselves in many instances from a reliance on tax dollars. In many western states the taxpayers are unable to keep up with the money expenses required to support these immigrants. Taxes continue to escalate to a point that is rapidly becoming unsustainable. It is not my intention to suggest, in any manner, that the new immigrants are not potentially a source of invigoration and renewal for our American experience. They generally are strongly interested in family, often spiritual, and typically are very hard workers.

The problem lies in the fact that liberals expect nothing and support dependency rather than encouraging assimilation into society which is troubling. In fact, in so many instances our tax dollars are used when we fail to rise up to resist illegal or unspiritual behaviors. This is something that is really worth considering. Things that quickly come to mind are social programs for those who equate want with need while not abided by the law. In many fundamental ways, such as being irresponsible regarding the financial and parental obligations for their off-springs is really our business. It is quite frankly unspiritual to believe that others should support you in these, and other similar instances. We are all obligated to carry our own weight and be personally responsible-or did I miss something while growing up?

We state, by our behaviors, that it doesn't affect us when the man fails to accept responsible for providing for their children. Further, now we are expected to serve as models and surrogate support systems due to this lack of moral outrage needed to confront the offenders who should be teaching their kids right from wrong. There was recently a federal program implemented just for this purpose which suggests that the federal government does not recognize a primary responsibility for the parent to be involved in giving their own children guidance and modeled appropriate adult behavior. We continue to pay into adulthood for these children due to the lack of learning these lessons often when they become our incarcerated inmates. Not only are we paying for the children of the irresponsible dad, we are supplying the needs of the mother who is forced to forego attempts to be self-sufficient due to the obligation to tend to the children.

In these instances, contrary to our assertions that it isn't our business, it really is. Due to the illogical nature of present-day society, the alternative to ineffectual parenting lacking in personal involvement is the abortion of off-springs. As the child cannot speak in their own defense and, since they do not have a vote in order to have power, their interests fail to receive appropriate consideration. Further, when we don't speak out about abortion we are further eroding the potential for our future as well. Life does not seem to be assessed with any intrinsic worth rather than the sums attached to satisfying nonspiritual needs.

With what has been estimated by some to be over 50 million babies terminated due to abortion. In effect, we have decimated close to 15% of our present population for the United States. They were our future wage earners who could have provided tax contributions. They could have been our military members and made our military more effective as our future leaders and inventors for which our future prosperity would have benefited. So when there is an abortion, it is your business. It affects each and every one of us in profound and intrinsic ways that cannot be denied. And when there are all forms of suffering in society that affects the functional basis of our society-the economy, criminal justice system, and education systems-it matters. How can any of us continue to bury our head in the sand and state that it doesn't affect me and, therefore, is none of my business? We are, in spite of our denial, our brother's keeper and will be held accountable by our Creator for the care we directed to the universal unit (as well as on an individual basis).

Unless we deny that our income comes from hourly exertion of sweat equity, then, they have to acknowledge that these things do affect them. The money that is taken away from our paychecks for the needs of others is made possible by our effort given to do a job. The paycheck did not come from thin air; it is the product of our spiritual responsibility to be productive and positively account for out time on earth by using our God-given abilities to accomplish work. This is done out of duty to our Creator to be self-sufficient and give a good accounting for ourselves. In the process of being spiritually appropriate, the result is that others receive a free ride while denying the obvious effect that their irresponsible behavior is having on us. But it is said that it is a free country and people are "free" to do what they want. Further insanity along this route exists when the leader of a political party suggests to Americans that they need to spend more time having fun and less time working. This idea that was expresses essentially was to do what is your passion. I believe that was how this idea was reported on the national news recently.

The actual cause of much of the unfettered amoral, unspiritual behavior that is in operation is the result of the self felt need for "individual freedom". This is the phase used to justify many behaviors referred to as desired by society. The use of the term individual freedom is another way of, in far too many instances, saying that we have license to ignore our spiritual responsibilities. These enacting bits of legislation that prescribes as acceptable a behavior are frequently specifically refused and considered repugnant in scriptural prose attributed to God. The perception that I gain from this line of legal reasoning is, as long as we are not hurting others and able to recognize the dangers of our proposed behavior, then we are free to do whatever we wish. We kill our off-springs before term, abuse our bodies, and engage in debauchery, gamble, and grant permission by legal codes to many means of scripturally immoral behavior. This is all under the guise of individual freedom. And practically every instance, these behaviors are not sanctioned by a Creator who only has our best interests at heart in prohibiting these behaviors. Do we not understand that there are limits to his patience and we cannot continually test him without the risk a response?

On the international level there is a general holy war in progress. Some have the belief in civilization being ruled by a sole religious law as the source of authority over all. They feel that those who dispute their beliefs are subject to death by, sometimes gruesome, means. As such many innocents are facing persecution and death. The religion that teaches love as the basis of our behavior are being brutally murdered and categorically slaughtered in fulfillment of scriptures and we tarry to acknowledge our Christian duty to protect our brethren while they are martyred. In the opposite vein, secular, humanistic society forwards the notion that religion is at the source of most ills of modern-day civilization. Spiritual individuals are perceived as sticks in the mud and who don't know how to have fun. In neither instance are we being served to a point of advancing our relationship with our Creator beneficially. We are only recently getting involved to address the zealot extreme beliefs with our very survival coming into question. This is due to idea that if it is not bothering us then we should just let them be. Now we are presented with the present war on terror. Our attention was aimed towards "fun" while the threat to our security expanded. By not getting involved, the results are than we are only now aware of the full extent of the danger that is upon us.

The ideas of being nonjudgmental with love and obedient to his instruction manual, is lost on the vast majority of secular individuals in present-day society. If you don't endorse their humanistic, secular progressive beliefs, you are marginalized within many professions due to alienation. The secular minority has reached majority membership within the ranks of many professional associations that provide the directives concerning practice. Now, their opinions and humanistic perspectives have been given the status of law within some state law codes. Further, you stand to be defamed with suggestions that personally held scriptural standards are inconsistent with their concepts of appropriate clinical practices. You may experience actual or perceived assaults to your personal character when you oppose their positions. Meanwhile, in our predominately secular society, the participation rates in religious activities typically find less than 1 of every 5 people in America actively involved. The only measurable exception is associated with occasional attendance for a special holiday or family event such as a wedding or funeral. We have forgotten our roots and abandoned our religious heritage that the America of our forefathers was based on. It has become blatant regarding the actual ambivalence towards religion. Legislation disallows prayer from many events such as athletic games and community-based meetings. I have seen undeserved angst expressed when the name of Jesus Christ spoken by so many people that I am truly puzzled. How can one attach negative connotations to someone who actually gave up his life for the benefit of humanity? Figure that out because I can't.

Meanwhile, a negative assessment of Islam is roundly criticized by our secular, tolerant society. Making any criticism can lead to being on what is the equivalent of a hit list by those who profess the faith I have seen reported by media. I don't see how the practice of murder for those who don't accept the faith when they live in some Islamic states is an enlightened lifestyle. Even though there is no religious freedom in those instances, the charge of intolerance is leveled from the liberal left if one dared to make a candid (and often accurate) comment about these practices. And this is primarily the current state of the practice of religion in America because we said that it wasn't our business just leave it alone. The obvious contradiction is that people who want to slander the precepts associated with our Christian faiths may do so-because it wasn't hurting them. In reality, a spiritual or religious person is seen as being ignorant and rigid, concrete in behavior and must be restricted whenever possible to avoid a need to consider the American heritage and values associated with that previous time. Meanwhile, our freedom of worship has been reserved for any religion other than Christianity in many instances-both in the media and in educational instructions.

So does it really matter if we think it is right or wrong for us to allow it to go on? Rather, are the alternatives we are presently experiencing so blatantly reprehensible to us that we give pause and consider where this is heading. We are going over the rapids and drowning ourselves without any exercises to preserve our way of life that is a great part of our heritage. This may not seem like a big deal to those who don't attend services or practice spiritual beliefs but it does serve as one example of how society has changed. It is remarkable that in the past 40+ years we find ourselves in this predicament where many don't know about this heritage and all that was sacrificed. Most came to these shores to be allowed to practice their faith. Now, the preference is to avoid the exercise of religious with this being the actual freedom that is asked for.

It seems that a choice of words makes all the difference to humans. In order to not have to seriously and critically consider something we just change the terminology associated with the thing. The idea is to attach an emotional response that allows it to not seem to be so bad. Further, the seemingly illogical preoccupation with word choice, instead of the total message conveyed is a sign of the continual deterioration of critical-thinking skills wherein the use of a single word is common practice in order to conjure up a picture instead having a logical, reasoned discussion. These restrictions on full expression serve to promote a resultant lack of civility and common-sense. This entire loss of expression making use and understanding of language as entirely directed to feelings (emotional reasoning) to promote actions is essentially "word salad" (my definition). The intent of this deviation of expression is to confuse, promote, defend, excuse, or any other means of promotion of self while disallowing the reality of facts to be the basis for decisions and actions.

Examples of how this a priori reliance on words, absent consideration of total content of what is under discussion, is used in secular society for words such as "love" or "fetus". In both of these instances the mere use of a different word has been employed to suggest a different, conflicting image. This is not, by long-held ideas, what is actually in consideration yet supports the use of spin and misdirection. So that we would not have to engage critical thinking, we have named the child while in the womb to be a fetus, thus suggesting that it not worthy of the classification as a human being. In this way it does not seem so harsh to abort the child. Concerning homosexual behavior (which if we consider that behavior as it actually consists of) we would find it repugnant, or at the least-not preferred, if we embraced traditional, conservative values. However, we are able to legislate into existence the union of those individuals due to the presentation that they have a right to now know "love". This is the rational as compared to rather concentrating on the practices associated the homosexual lifestyle and scriptural prohibitions. The additional word that further allows for this legislation is the word "individual freedom" and has added legitimacy to the interest of codifying of homosexual unions. The fact that the use of heterosexual denotes a benefit of continuation of the human race where homosexual does not provide any like utility appears to be lost on the federal judicial system. Due to these words and an avoidance of consideration for more traditional, scriptural guidance as to the purpose of the union to go forth and multiply-we now have the battle over homosexual rights. It bears noting that some psychological existential literature suggested that the term love was originally conjured up to make more palatable the primitive drive associated with human procreation. In this instance it does not even apply to its' latest use.

Not only is the alteration of more blatant wording used to avoid dealing with others. Generally, we have four primary ways to address problems. We avoid the problem, we ignore the problem, we deny the problem on some level, or we deal with the issue. Usually, the first step is to avoid the issue first until such time as it insults our sense of right and wrong that we must do something. Then, we either deny that is really a problem that needs work or change the wording about what is going on to make it seem less offensive. This leads to a period of time when the problem further festers and marinades. A serious assault on the morality of the people in the society puts the issue to the forefront and, only then, are we motivated to deal with it. In the recent past this process has led to making the behavior okay legally in order to avoid confrontation and conflict between people in the community. This is possible because of the adage of "if it is not any of my business, then I will just leave it alone and let them do what they want to". After all, "it's not hurting anything is it?" This entire process plays out on a reoccurring basis for every major issue that has led us further and further away from our moral roots and scriptural instructions. In my early life, being principled was considered a positive personality trait. Now, if you have issue with anyone doing practically anything you are considered mean-spirited for having expectations for conduct.

People say that things have always been as bad as they are now. It appears compelling to state that this is not an accurate assessment of our time. The most basic aspects of society are being challenged and fundamentally muted or refuted by secular individuals who have no apparent respect for God's design. The family as consisting of the two gender makeup, the ability of the parent to raise their own children, expectations of personal responsibility while working rather than receiving a handout, the value and sanctity of life, the right to live for all human creation, the responsibility to respect others, and being obedient to our Creator's rules and design for living are all assaulted. This short list covers the most fundamental and all-encompassing aspects that have been at the core of civilization over 6 thousand years ago at the dawn of recorded history. And, in the past 4 decades we have attempted to undo all of it. All because we had the position, that if it doesn't affect us we should just ignore it. The essential result being that those elements who do not share values formed from our onset were ignored. They have been allowed to take the world where it should have never even considered.

At issue here is actually, "Are we willing to be ruled by such ambivalent disregard for spiritual, scriptural guidance and accept those things that we don't like"? Essentially, because we didn't endure conflict to deal with those who conduct I did not approve of. If we don't actively address things that we personally disagree with, we are inviting being forced to accept and embrace immorality at a future date. So it is a question of making the decision of, "Do I deal with it now while it is manageable"? Or, "Do I let it get out of hand", and become the "way it is" over of my future objections. Remember, it will affect you or those who are important to you at some point. The only person to blame, when forced to endure what we oppose, is your own self. The most serious fear we should endorse is in the receipt of a punishment from our Creator. I fully anticipate that it will be serious and painful due to our lack of taking a responsible interest in our world. We failed to show the strength to address the ills that plague us when they are unpleasant because it was a distraction away from our needs being met.

When we, as a nation, sanctify behaviors that are repugnant to our Creator we are inviting his judgment. This places us in a very unsafe situation without a benefit as there is no excuse for our disinterest. Scripture speaks to the judgment of the Creator over his chosen people when they refused to obey his guidance and, in that instance, they went for practically 2 thousand years without a home. They were gathered together in the late 1940 and have returned home into the present. It cannot be considered good to experience the punishments for failure to comply and history that is not acknowledged and studied will be repeated. Certainly it will be to the pain of those whose ignorance allowed for the repeat. I firmly believe that there is not much left to be made permissible to invite the judgment of God. Our rebellion is such that our replication of our previous conditions comparable to other civilizations that ignored moral and spiritual truisms has occurred. When we, as a nation, legalize immoral behaviors we will be judged as a nation. My fear is that, as a final affront to human decency, we will begin taxing religious organizations and houses of worship. Further, we will also legislate in favor of permissible sexual conduct between adult and adolescent. It seems impossible to consider that these things could happen. However, did it not also seem impossible 30 years ago to suggest that homosexual marriage would be condoned and put into legal codification? No one would have believed it then, why are my fears any more unrealistic in the future?

Chapter Six

Isn't It All About Power?

It Is Really About Getting Your Way

It is common in social settings such as a school, work, and community to consider who is in charge as a source of much conversation, disagreement, and conflict. In introductory collegiate political science courses, the subject of East versus West, North versus South, or Industrial versus Non-Industrial were at the focus of much treatment to describe the status of the world and its' people. The essential consideration is that the conflict between peoples has a primary basis over the competition for the use of scares resources. The desire to have an advantage in ownership of those resources has been the origins of world conflict since the beginnings of kingdoms. Finally, the divergence between those of various cultures and nationalities is the origins for the basis of differences in outlook and worldview. And, this has led to the various geopolitical systems that direct the world's population into the modern era.

This divergence has included the ideals associated with the principles of multiculturalism and diversity. The central theme involves an acceptance of multiplicity of worldviews and acting distinctly different based upon a divergent worldview. Theoretically, there is no wrong and, conversely, all cultures are right in concurrence with their own shared cultural values and beliefs. The end result of this is the suggestion of considering our world from a subjective perspective absent universal, absolutes of conduct that all must observe. It follows that this perspective is in opposition to collectivism. The reality of God's law, as being of universal application and relative and appropriate to all people without difference due to the time continuum of our civilization, is placed in question by this principle. We have begun traveling down a slippery slope when we allow for behaviors based upon a preference for national consensus. A more appropriate preference should include the principles and ideals that are provided by scriptural truisms. God's law is appropriate for all people, at all times, and in all countries. All individual values should be considered and formed based upon his directions rather than being based upon human imperfections and self-serving interests. Various ages have led to new ways of living as is evidenced by the past 50+ years. The upheaval and conflict of those years weren't addressed based on a primary reliance on the ideals of a spiritual origin. Outcomes were based on court decisions and corrective actions from a secular perspective.

Examples of how we pander to various cultural groups in this country, rather than acknowledging that our problems affect all and everyone's interests are equally valid. Problems associated with use of our language, availability of benefits, and allowances made for some rather than all have become a national issue. I should not have to press

"2" on my push tone keypad of my telephone to hear English. The English language has been the language in use for over 400 years in America. Why are we now providing preferential treatment for our Hispanic immigrants instead of expecting them to learn the language that has been in use since the United States was founded? All previous immigrants were required to "assimilate" but now secular progressives suggest that this is somehow insensitive and hostile to our newly arrived applicants for citizenship. It is not a complaint of our newest immigrants by any means. Treating anyone differently is counterproductive to developing unity as a country. This will be a problem unless corrected. Further, why do we allow students with substandard accomplishments (when compared with other applicants) preferred acceptance to our colleges and universities based on the color of their skin? Meanwhile, we exclude students who are in competition with them who have superior academic records in comparison. Again-why the preferential treatment? We are all in this experience as one and our unity is more important that the competition we share. There are no black issues, white issues, or brown issues. Instead, there are issues which we need to collectively roll up our sleeves over and handle as a unit. If we refuse to do so, we will splinter and fight between ourselves to our own national undoing.

We have to go beyond our simple-minded way of viewing ourselves based on making sense of our environment by classifying others in various ways for ease of identification. The more complex, yet unappreciated and ignored, reality is that whether one is "black" or "white" or any other skin pigment does not change vital facts of life. We bleed the same blood, have the same heart beating, shared the same needs and ambitions; while each of us need acceptance, understanding, and a human love from mutual appreciation. Every person on the planet, disregarding racial classification, is an equal child of God. The love he has for all of us is expected to be mirrored by us for each other.

This is our obligation to mirror the love as demonstrated by the one who made us. The tears I shed for my own family in times of pain I also shed for others without consideration of race; otherwise, we will ensure the continued deterioration of our world until the mutual intolerance and hatred will be our destruction as a planet.

Why does a racial group that feels the need to march in the streets and riot for tolerance or acceptance for themselves, fail to also riot for the perceptions of injustice for others? Behaving without the same attitude for other racial groups is suspect and is just as racially discriminate. A communist philosopher stated, over 100 years ago, that America would fall from within without any outside interference and it appears possible that this was a very astute observation. However, it is not only our cultural clashes and lack of adherence to the principle of collectivism that may doom the constitutional experiment. Our hostility, based upon gender with the inherent inequity of power, also leads to a further fracturing of our social fabric.

A very disturbing fact that I read while accomplishing my master's program was that, throughout the world, over 70% of women had experienced verbal, physical, or sexual violence against them by the male counterparts who were in their lives. It could be a father, grandfather, uncle, brother, husband, or neighborhood male. Nevertheless, the desire to have their wishes and desires met by the female gender was such that males resorted to abuse to gain the submission of the physically, weaker female. This represents a fundamental power inequity and is at the individual basis for the misuse of power and exercise of non-spiritual ideals. It never was the intention of our Creator to have a lack of honor for any of his creation. I believe that he has always wanted us to cherish each other and look out for each other with civility. If our beliefs and ideals are not sound, the use of force against others will not make them any more legitimate or appropriate. This misuse of power and the conflict that exists has not ceased since antiquity when one brother killed the other, and continues on to now. Inhumanity between male and female, different cultural entities, and suspicions based on differences has been going on since we first settled the shores. My personal awareness of this conflict was of the beginning of the 1960's which turned out to be a very turbulent era in American history. In some ways, this was the beginning salvo to our present host of unresolved issues that were never competently addressed.

Initially, as a child of the 60's and 70's the civil rights movement that has been central to my life was never far from the boiling point in society. Racial hatred has served to block many attempts at uniting our people throughout history in this and other countries. It is always associated with being in power and having control over the limited resources available. At present, it is the case of being cognizant of the needs of the Hispanic population in America and the rights of these immigrants into the U.S. No matter how things change over the centuries, they remain the same as the question of power, who has it, who wants it, and to what extent people will try to either keep it or take it away from those who have it persists. Elementary political science lessons state that the world and its people endure conflict over the inherent competition over limited resources. This is the case, rather than devising a system to equitably share what our Creator has provided for our use and stewardship.

The minority population segment in any given society is usually attempting to promote their agenda and believe that the majority segment should accept the minority position. There exists a desire to assimilate those beliefs into the culture with a new cultural face being the actual result of assimilation. The actual fact is that the minority wants their way and to have their wishes predominate in the operation of the society when honestly acknowledged. This desire exists even though they are the less populace number. This is problematic because, even though their ideas and principles may be worthy and desirable, the majority is likely going to avoid acceptance of these minority ideals. Cultural differences and divergent beliefs over government, law, school, benefits, etc. all transpire to make this very difficult if not likely. Without the evidence of much social upheaval and unrest brought to bear by the minority that is dissatisfied with their lesser status, no change occurs. In this country, the tyranny of the majority or so it is described in much literature associated with political thought, is harnessed and controlled with the actual end result being that minority positions are given equal footing. This is attempted even though they represent a lesser number of the overall population total. In fact, the minority position is supported and codified into law by liberal judges who often support their interests. Their decisions give the minority position a preferred status legally even when a vast majority is completely in opposition. It may be argued otherwise, yet in political and social operation, the minority points of view are reaching a privileged status legally as the outcome of the recent and current legal decisions in America. These decisions determine a legal code significantly absent spiritual principles in some fundamental ways.

This muting of national consensus-where minority positions are preeminent represents an example of perversion of power. The primary dysfunction lies in its inability to satisfy the majority needs and demands within that society. This is the central social problem that will divide the nation due to a future push from the many demanding to have control returned. This is as compared to the present, with the few dictating their will. As such, it is the opposite extreme of repression by the majority and is a misuse of power by those tasked with interpretation of the law. Present legal standards appear to have a basis that is from such a sterile, compulsive mindset that they refuse the historical customs and traditions. Instead, decisions are derive with amoral views arrived at by overthinking the issue while avoiding basic human, moral, common-sense considerations. The majority does not endorse this vanilla interpretation of precedent that avoids acknowledgment of our traditions and values. There is a central issue to account for this state of affairs which is a lack of moral considerations. The legal consideration at the basis of judicial review appears to equate moral ideation from scriptural prose as being associated with rigid, inflexible and somehow uninformed bumpkins. They are suspected of having an attitude lacking in intelligence that is certainly not on par with present-secular, "educated" beliefs and standards. What I perceive as arrogance and conceit attitudes serves to insulate them from everyday people who they supposes need to be lead into more modern, hip reality. This reality supposes that a rational, moral understanding is insensitive, harsh, and hostile to the human condition.

Present-day law presupposes that you cannot legislate based upon morality and has developed legal decisions have gone to an opposite extreme of disregarding moral considerations in the promulgation of law and public policy. In one of my initial law courses of many years ago, the foundational material clearly underscored the judicial practice of excluding morality and spiritual traditions from law interpretation and formation. In spite of our moral heritage as the basis for criminal conduct this was the current practice of judgeships at the federal level. A case in point is that in approximately 70% of the states of the United States (until federal judges ruled otherwise) the majority of the citizens of those states, or in other instances, the majority of the lawmakers within the state assemblies have placed within the state constitutions prohibitions against gay marriage. This infers the choice of the people. It follows the principle of government "of the people" and "by the people" with their desires being acknowledged within the law code.

However, under the guise of "individual freedom", federal circuit court judges have thrown out these state constitutional amendments as unconstitutional while ignoring the values of the majority. This misuse of power excluded scriptural-based ideals and perverts the sensibilities of those who realize the amoral considerations associated with same-sex marriages. The unintended and illegitimate use of the institution of marriage that was originated from the beginning of time based upon our Creator's prescription (if one believes scriptural explanations) made legally permissible by, what I believe is, a misuse of power through federal judge impropriety.

In order to highlight the ignorance of a position that believes that the development and evolution of the American legal system should be absent morality based on scripture, consider this. The fundamental, and arguably initial, Judeo-Christian foundational code which is popularly known as the Ten Commandments is at the heart of western civilization (includes universally recognized ideals). This initial pronouncement states that murder is not allowed, slander is unlawful, suggested fraudulent activities such as false witness are prohibited, etc. (you get the general idea). These principles are enshrined in our legal codes and are the basis of judicial actions regarding what is expected "right conduct". So, on one hand, to claim that morality is not the basis for law is absurd. On the other hand, the suggestion of this lack of standing in the formulation of law for moral ideals, is nothing less than an expression of legal determinations. It is based upon progressive, secular liberalism that fundamentally places man as authority of right and wrong. This state of legal theory ignores, diminishes, and marginalizes the cultural and spiritual heritage of our nation's development out of preference for the evolution of science and humanism as the modern-day state of America. In short, we are god and make up what is permissible and God's expressed standards of morality are incompatible with this modern-day perception of relevance. In effect, this is being suggested by such an attitude by legal minds who promote decisions that don't come from an appropriate consideration of moral traditions.

Equally, I have seen statistics that indicate that a figure approaching close to 70% of Americans do not believe in unfettered abortion. They point to the need for specific instance to be present to allow for an abortion. Either an instance of incest, rape, or potential threats to the life of the mother is deemed necessary as a precondition for abortions to occur. Others suggest that a deformities of the unborn as sufficient cause. Nevertheless, a vocal minority of secular individuals have ensured the continuation of abortion on demand in many localities by buffaloing legislators to gain the practice. Frequently, they are supported by liberal judges (who refute spiritual considerations) based on precedent established from the court decision of Roe vs. Wade. Further, our government provided financial resources to organizations that are engaged in the promotion of the act of abortion (appropriated for "education services"). The end results is that there is spending of federal funds to support facilities that, in some instances, are acting in a manner that is spiritually troubling.

Spiritually, it can be said that we are supposed to get along and live together in the sight of our Creator while having connectedness, collectiveness, and sensitivities to each other's needs, hopes, and aspirations. We are intended to be a blessing to each other and not a stumbling block. Together we are to seek the kingdom of God and gain eternal admittance. Only in those instances when scripture is clear in its directions, is single-mindedness appropriate as the yardstick regarding what is moral and appropriate, otherwise it would be more appropriate to be, first and foremost, a blessing. This does not suppose ignoring or accepting amoral behaviors without notice, rather, we still show love and demonstrate patient hope for an individual's awakening. Unfortunately, as I have alluded to there are a great many times when the term "versus" gets in the way of achieving a truly blessed relationship with each other.

On one hand, there is a leader who recently gained the ability to destroy at a great cost. He expressed a desire regarding having the entire male population of his country with the same hair style as himself. I don't know where his head is at and can't figure it out? This is certainly not the mature thinking that I would anticipate for someone who may call for a nuclear launch. Another leader wants an empire and his delusional desire for empire may end up putting the world at war with countless millions of innocent people slaughtered due to his apparent ego-driven desires. There is a belief that his desire for empire is based on a dream of greatness for his legacy once gone. Here again, it is troubling that the world's peace can be affected by such a mind. I wonder if his achievement of empire, if successful, will add one day to his life or one inch to his height. It just seems so utterly a waste of the world that God has provided us with.

No matter how you look at it, power continues to come into play and rear its' ugly head. It is important to understand the dichotomy relationship associated with power. This requires looking at the having, versus the not having, of that power while asking whether it is important to consider the human needs. Having power ultimately appears to allow people to feel important and since they have a monopoly on the truth, power is needed to ensure that their truth is enforced. Logic suggests to this author that having the power allows for one to see to it that their interpretation of life and truth is observed and adhered to. This brings comfort and satisfaction to that person and stability to their psyche as they typically see themselves as being sensible and intelligent and not having misguided ideas. Otherwise, if they would think that they were not living in a manner that was appropriate or correct and they did not have the power to control their destiny then there would be inner conflict associated with their self-esteem. In short, people see themselves as reasonable and intelligent; not doing things their way is unacceptable thus the need for power to enforce their sensibilities.

This thinking is generally incongruent to leading a truly free, spiritual existence as the only one we fully have control over is our self. Having power over oneself is at the center of the beginning stages of the development of a spiritual existence; having power over others is a dangerous deviation away from finding peace and spiritual contentment. There will always be example of ongoing struggles to maintain that control. And taking it a step further, the act of achieving complete spiritual freedom is to acknowledge that we don't even have control over ourselves. Rather we are molded by our Creator as he deems appropriate if we truly sacrifice our free will for the benefit of an intimate, meaningful relationship with our God that ensures eternal security. It requires obedience and compliance to God's wishes and does not allow for excuses and twisting of scriptural prose to fit a misguided and immoral behavioral pattern or belief system.

As already alluded to; the quest for obtaining, or effort to retain, power is at the heart of conflict. One only need look at the world at any given time to see that we have been in conflict since the beginning of recorded history. There are many who have had temporal power grabs throughout history. In every instance they fell to a new, more militarily advanced foe. The only time that power has been obtained short of bloodshed was from a social revolution by a spiritual leader. It has been possible, throughout history, to identify times when the actions of a spiritual leader changed the landscape of attitudes and perspectives. Christ has forever emboldened us with the idea that love conquers all. Even to the present many practice and believe in this ideal. Truly finding that love for humankind is important to development a relationship with God and, it tends to be a life-long pursuit. It remains elusive and may not ever be fully achieved without mistakes and stumbles along the way.

It bears awareness to consider the attempts of those in power in non-traditional fields as they impact our lives greatly. The press and media use marketing to manipulate people to purchase their products. The marketers who peddle their products in the media frequently portray the unusual in society as the "norm" and thereby ignoring the reality their ads do not represent the public accurately. They focus on the exceptions rather than the rule; how many female race car drivers are there but they are receive a disproportionate amount of attention. This is in comparison to the majority profile of a race car driver that is typically male. (I do not know of an instance where the object of the media attention actually won a major race-yet those who have won the race are ignored due to a preference for the unusual). How many female drummers are there? There are probably much fewer females drumming that there are male drummers. Those extreme or minute examples of the population groupings are shown on the commercial rather than portraying the norm. An athlete, taken in the last round of the draft, receives news coverage for what appears to be based on his sexual orientation rather than any meaningful reference to any special skills and ability on the field. The presentation of characters in commercials that fail to represent majority norms and fail to represent the dynamics of society are liberal-minded attempts to repaint our culture as they wish it to be. Further, the idea is to concentrate on squeezing every available dollar from any segment of the population (whether they have the money or not) in order to maximize their market share. As such, every means is acceptable as it confirms these objectives.

The obvious interpretation that this writer has determined to be the case for those in marketing is that they are trying to impress on society their interpretation of what society is supposed to be by their standards.

They view a world that is far removed from the reality of our existence and attempt to direct people towards their worldview. Much of what they portray is liberalism in its most basic form. There is an idealistic nature to the scenes that belies rational thought. It is very important to consider the actual power that has been demonstrated by marketing over the past 50+ years as phenomenal. No aspect of society is exempt from their twist at what they believe to be right and good. Often, it is not in our best interests as we have become so predisposed to consume, and less interested more spiritual positions that are not associated with materialism. Their marketing schemes appear not to be genuinely related to the reality of an existence of spirituality nature. Instead, they represent a portion of the hedonistic, materialistic component of the present reality.

Should one dispute the impact of marketing on our collective lives they only need do the math to discover the full weight of marketing's interference us. Most individuals are firmly connected to their televisions with a few others being dependent on radio. With each of these entertainment choices, the average ratio of the actual show time to advertising is equally split. This time is spent attempting to sell us something, or in some other way pushing a position or belief onto us. This adds up to a very large portion of the day being bombarded by a sales pitch. They use of sophisticated research to try to devise intensive and effective means of gaining our adherence to purchases or positions that they are forwarding. It is accurate to surmise that a large amount of time and money is spent to influence us. Thus, it is foolish to ignore the impact wielded by those in marketing on our lives. As marketing's methods are dependent on using the media to affect us, the media is also worthy of considering for the impact on our lives that they exert.

The media appears to have a demonstrated preference for a specific political attitude and a commonly expressed thought is that democratic, liberal party beliefs receive larger attention in a vast majority of the cases. This results in the slanting of the news due to favorably reporting. In essence, the media presentation has the tendency to impact under-educated and less informed viewers in a manner that may have an effect favorable for liberal, social policy. As an end result, there occurs an impact on who are, or become, the power players in society. Rather than seriously addressing the responsibility inherent with the opportunity to provide information to the populace, it may be all about impact. It becomes an attempt to influence rather than educate or to editorialize rather than inform. This represents an abuse of the relationship that necessarily exists between the media and the mainstream viewer. This does not mean that the tendency is rampant over all stations and broadcasts, yet a sufficient impact to have a derogatory effect to society has resulted. This misuse of the power inherent in presenting information by demonstrating with the use of a slanted approach to journalism can only be redirected by tuning out.

Other entities experience an enticement to use their responsibilities to wield power rather than be reverent of their inherent inequity over others. Nowhere is this truer than in the educational system. We spend more money than practically any nation in the world on our educational system yet we are well below others with our meager results in student proficiency. In comparison to other nations around the globe who do not possess our resources, we lag behind. I have seen the basic ineptitude in my dealings in instances as common as within an exchange with a general store clerk in a convenience store. The younger cashier is unable to make change, figure the total, and produce accurate representations of the purchase and return of the excess money given towards the purchase. It is so amusing that a calculator is needed to figure basic four mathematical operations. (I don't believe that these individuals could identify what these operations even are).

When the present student cannot tell time when looking at a dial watch (not digital readout) or make change for a purchase I wonder what the school system is actually teaching them. After all, how many students will utilize calculus after leaving school in practically any instance? Most probably never, although this is preferred to those previously provided lessons in the school systems such as deportment, ethics, learning respect and cultivating critical thinking. Presently, it a common experience for me during each day to be exposed to situations where advanced reasoning is either not present or underutilized. I frequently encounter a general lack of ability to "connect the dots" so as to speak as it relates to drawing conclusion with demonstrated intelligence that results in solid, thoughtful considerations.

The explanation for this lack of cognitive demonstration can be found in the reality that a recognized portion of individuals do not develop fully the skills associated with rational thought. They often do not operate beyond the theorized, third stage of reasoning which has been referred to as concrete-operational thinking. They demonstrate normative-based communications that center on "should", "ought", or "must" which may have their origins from subjective, emotional rationalizations. Frequently they do not benefit from educated guidance as youths and this leads to failing to fully develop adequate problem-solving skills. This is necessary in order to develop novel approaches to difficult circumstances which involve considering sometimes obscure evidence that is not readily obvious. The fundamentally lost skill involves being able to learn information and, then-apply what they learned to things that don't seem obvious and require novel applications. The point to be made concerning this is that the present, public educational system does not seem to be equipping the students to use rational-deductive methods that are complex and advanced in their use. I believe that we truly wish to promote the inhabitant's ability to function and use their God-given gifts and talents. Therefore, it is imperative that we avoid spoon-feeding information and data to our youths for the primary purpose of passing a government-required test. We need to concentrate on providing our future generation with the skills needed to do great things for the benefit of humanity. We must teach them in a manner that requires the application of scriptural principles to come to decisions about life's issues as well. This is what occurs when one uses what has been referred to as spiritual intelligence (something that is rapidly being lost to prosperity due to lack of attention).

Once the student arrives at the collegiate system of education, liberal-minded perspectives are the norm at the expense of a well-rounded debate as left-wing agendas are more popular and established. In some instances, they are the only agendas supported while conservative students may not fully experience favorable support on par with their liberal peers. My previous political science training provided me with an understanding that conservative agendas develop with advanced age and experience of the individual in many instances. This serves as the counterbalance to this propensity for liberalism that is expressed in many school settings and more prevalent with younger, minority, and some middle-aged adults. At present, this push-pull mentality concerning public opinion of conservatism versus liberalism is in an on-going tilt from one to the other as the means of government with liberalism in vogue by the educated elite. Meanwhile, conservatism is popular among non-college educated, rural folks, or those who stand to lose financially due to adverse governmental tax rates. This is generally because some statistics that I have seen support the idea that higher wage earner are often prone to be conservative in their personal politics. (Obviously this does not account for the strictly party line voters). The problem is that those who are not politically sophisticated are being led with misinformation and confrontation of a political system that is broken. We are rendering to the government our tax money but are not having our interests represented-rather we serve as a depository of funds to support the liberal, expanses of government out of control. This represents the fullest extent of the overreach of power and may prove fatal unless curbs to the purse strings of our elected officials are forthcoming. In short, government exercises the most lethal and overarching power in this country and generally, around the world.

What I have personally see happen, in effect, is that as most managers and individuals in positions of authority in practically every major area of the work force and government has a college degree. These degrees were attained by attendance and efforts, in large part, by the liberal majority that educate the college student body. Further, when these individuals enter the work force they emulate their superiors and embrace the supervisor's opinions and plans if they wish to gain favor and subsequent promotions is often the case. What results is that liberal-minded ideals become the basis for company policy that is formulated from the top of the organization and, in what seems to be an increasing number of instances, God is not part of the equation as to the actual operation of the business in what seems to be a vast majority of instances. This is not totally true-there are spiritual individuals in all areas of the workforce. It is getting harder to find them is my experience. Secular humanistic attitudes control the supervision of the workforce and frequently fail to promote or advance those who do not share secular values. Based on the psychological principle of having preference for similarity, the end result is that advancement by favoritism occurs rather than more traditional ideal of my youth. Now reward is connected to having shared ideals rather than primarily based on knowledge, experience, and skills. The end result is that liberalism receives an undeserved control over the livelihood of many. Those in the workforce are forced to sacrifice their personal morality in fundamental ways for the benefit of the dollar in order to survive economically. In short, their soul is subject to sale due to the financial necessities of present-day, secular society and they may be forced to sacrifice full experiencing of career development for their spiritual values and beliefs.

Christ stated that we were to "render to Caesar what is Caesar's and render to God what is God's". Presently, our government and its leaders continue to press for more and more from the people. They fashion laws that attacks the faith of the believers and calls it, among other things, either individual freedom or "income redistribution". The traditional belief that hard work lead to success has been replaced with hard work means more available tax money to provide for those who do not often choose to work. Each year leads to a new program from government to provide financial means to the citizenry. But, where is it coming from? Presently, those who are successful are attacked as not like us. They are pitted against a majority of individuals who haven't been as successful. The results are that animosity exists with our country rapidly turning into a state of the "haves" versus the "have not's". Being successful is made to be a bad thing and just getting by leads to reward from government in the form of financial handouts. Present policy gives hard work a bad name.

In further consideration and to serve as an added development of the discussion over government spending, an essential thought must be shared. As a constitutional government we are, theoretically, guided by the U.S. Constitution and our elected officials are obligated to be compliant with it. This initial document makes specific note within the preamble that we are to "provide for the common defense, promote the general welfare" etc. This does not clearly and specifically indicate the implications that programs may be established which are, by their guidelines, designed for certain subgroups of society. The general welfare, as I perceive it, is to give provisions for all people, equally.

It an additional point to understand that human nature is such that when they are given a benefit they are frequently grateful for that gift. It follows that, reasonably, they will reciprocate in favor of the one who gave them the advantage. I do believe that elected officials are primarily guided by an interest in helping those who they serve. The problem remains that the money that is available from taxpayers serves an available temptation to be used strategically to marshal a plurality to remain in office. The taxes available provide the means to push for projects, programs, or facility and staff funding which is, based on human nature, beneficial if approached properly.

In order to avoid having this suspicion supported, it would be reasonable to legislate with the interest of all rather than that of a specific, identified subgroup or subclass. The object of the program, the design of the program, the eligibility requirements, and preference for promoting dependence has the results of some being excluded. This is a direct, detrimental strategy that government has devised unintentionally, yet is cause of a less than responsible approach to securing all of the people's mutual rights to share resources. Further, it serves a basis for strategy so as to allow for the realization of my just previously expressed suspicions. As such, it represents a part of the problem towards our present insolvent federal financial crisis. Further, it demonstrates how spending can result in achieving political party power. Finally, I believe that the elected officials are, generally speaking, intelligent and handle their personal financial affairs in a way that ensure a continuing profit and expansion of personal income. Compare this to the state of the federal budget deficit and it bears asking a question. "How are their own finances handled in such a way as to ensure that they will be in good shape while the nation teeters on bankruptcy?" This is puzzling to me-I just don't understand how it is appropriate for the people of the nation to be put in a position that could result in utter chaos and unimaginable distress. In contrast, my perception of the elected official's personal considerations of their own financial resources include assumption that they are better handled to allow for reasonable comfort.

Where does it end? There is a country adage that goes something like this, "you can't get blood out of a turnip". Swiftly, that is what it is coming to in western civilization. One need look to the movements of people in some high tax states in this country or the high tax rates of the federal system. Those of financial means are leaving high tax states or areas. Granted, a few have much of the wealth but, unless they achieved their status by illegal gain, then they should not have to apologize for being a success. They have expending their efforts towards the accumulation of wealth and should not have to make excuses. I feel that liberals suggest, based on their actions, that scripture infers that people would be spiritually sound by giving up what they have for charity for the masses. This is a weak interpretation of scripture. In reality, more often when liberals employ scriptural principles, they use what supports spin absent full scriptural interpretation. Alms giving is required, yet the sacrifice of honestly earned capital beyond a reasonable proportion set aside for our neighbor, is not endorsed scripturally. For liberals the definition of what makes up a reasonable portion is debatable. Even after giving, in some individuals situations, more than half of the earned income for taxes-it is not seen as providing a "fair share".

Chapter Seven

God Is Only Meant To Be First

What about That Didn't You Understand?

There are a number of ways in which to determine what is important to someone. How the person spends their time or their money are but two primary means determining what is of value to someone. If something is of high value, then one will spend in a manner that allows them to retain enough money to be able to afford the product. They will go without other essential items so that they can buy the desired item. What is a problem at present is that there often exists misplaced value which is demonstrated by having money used for pleasure-related items while doing without essentials for living. This is evident for the gambler or addict who gamble or abusive substances with their available resources in order to feed this addictive behavior.

And it is not just how the individual places importance on items of dubious worth that can be problematic. How society values things impacts what behaviors that the person can legally demonstrate. One can look at the laws of the land to ascertain what is considered important based on the attention that they give to the item. What the individual values are as they relate to what society allows (and what is prohibited) goes a great way towards showing the relative value that those in power have for the individual and life issues or rights. It is increasingly apparent that what God states as the model for living is not what present-day society determines to have legitimacy. Our laws state that a female can determine the fate of her unborn child; not that life is sacred. The scriptural prose that discusses the lot of womankind stated that they were to bring the child to term as prescribed at the time that the first inhabitants were turned out of the Garden of Eden. In this instance, secular preferences prevail. I have also read the claim that the new Affordable Care Act will make use of panels for eligibility determinations. They will theoretically be tasked with determining whether one will receive (cost effective) medical treatment or be denied life-saving or life-extending efforts. In this instance, money seems to be more a value that human life. So it appears to me that it is being suggested that the most vulnerable, (the very young and the elderly) are seen as having subjective value that is determined by people rather than the Creator.

Another look at laws in the nation find that pornography and gambling are now at a place of continually expanding acceptance by an ever increasing portion of the population. Common news article report more casinos and gambling activities that are becoming available to many jurisdictions in the country. The idea appears to be that our work efforts and sweat equity are not the only accepted means to gain income. To an ever-increasing level, a game of chance is considered a reasonable way to gain income. No longer is money earned primarily through honest toil by some people. Further, rather than put in the effort into the cultivation of an intimate, loving relationship based upon shared opinions, values, and ideals; many look at a magazine to view the naked body. This results in leaves nothing to the imagination and seems to circumvent the incredibly personal, special experience when an intimate relationship fully is known. In neither of these instances, pornography or gambling, can it be said that they are only recent arrivals to society. They have been around since early days of civilization. A truly civilized society does not accept this debauchery. To debase the body and make it a public spectacle seems to me to be somehow immodest and lacking in reverence to the personal nature associated with privacy that is based on my conservative, Christian-based upbringing. It is, nevertheless, a sizeable financial enterprise in the country to purchase pictures of perceived attractive bodies. Concerning gambling, the money generated by this debasement actually covering the cost of education in many states to a significant degree. Possibly the scriptural adage that money, as evil as it is, can be used for good is in application in this instance. The actual state of the education being provided is a topic for reasonable debate as to its effectiveness and questioning whether the money is well-spent.

How money is utilized is another topic to determine what is important. We spend primarily on food, housing, electronic gear, leisure and entertainment, and on substances. These substances allow the users to avoid reality while being susceptible to all kinds of ill while intoxicated and in altered states. This does not mean that everyone does this, others have divergent priorities that may include God. It just seems to be harder and harder to find individuals who tithe 10% of their income to a church. More often, many waste their resources on the nonessentials of life for the purposes of pleasure and escapes from reality.

In an earlier time when tithing was common place, churches provided support to many people (they still a great deal of good often). When considering the shift in spending that is now used to purchase spirits and drugs, the result is that people's interest are now directed at pleasure rather that to support churches efforts to help people. The new reality is that people gain assistance from taxpayer-funded, governmental, welfare to secure the needs of the poor. They tax for a figure coming close to half of money making up the gross income of some wage earner to support these social spending programs. Rather than consider the largess of this system, elected officials continue to demonstrate a vain belief that they know better what we need than we do. They continue to believe the answer is to have more programs. I am confused as to why the government think they are entitled to as much as 40% (or more) of our income when God only required 10% of our first fruits? In so many ways already described, as well as in other ways not even considered, the secular view of the world forms the basis for how we must live. This suggests that funding lavish government spending, escape from reality with substances, debauchery, and a lack of respect and value for life are the preferred basis for our existence. This has replaced a preference for our origins.

The factual issue that has occurred by this change from church to government for provision is that now people's "god" is the government. This is the loss of a reliance on the spiritually–based faith groups and organizations who also forwarded spiritual ideals and scriptural education to individuals at a former age. This situation not only allowed for favorable experiences of being helped, it also allowed for development of faith and spiritual growth that is now gone. These groups were at the heart of financial support for many in an earlier time prior to the advent of the government programs of support and the funding. Now, due to the resultant lack of interaction between those who advance spiritual concerns and issues and a turn to secular government for support has led to a general ignorance of even the most basic tenants of the Christian faith. In most instances, this is due to a lack of association. Further, misunderstandings are common now due to a complete misrepresentation of scripture that is done so as to twist scriptural prose to advance their agendas. It is common to see individuals misquote or blatantly misstate scripture to support their positions on issues affecting the citizens of the country so that they can gain an advantage thru a spinning of our Creator's plans and expectations. In some instances, individuals make deliberate attempts at distortion of scripture prose that the populace is unable to recognize due to their lack of knowledge of spiritual beliefs. Thus, misrepresentation allows for those who are not fundamentally engaged in the political process to be misguided to provide support. I would not have believed that evil would use a contorted application of the very words of the Creator as a means of separating his creation from him towards a demise that will have no return.

So how do we spend our time? When I was a young adult or late teenager my father admonished me to avoid "spending all that time in front of the idiot box". What he was referring to was the television. Times have continued to evolve since then and now smart phones, computers, and so many electronic gadgets have found their way into mainstream society. Now there is figuratively more than one idiot box with many divergent possibilities to take up the time, energy, and motivation of the individual. This allows them to escape from facing life and being keenly aware of how they (and many others) are avoiding the important things. Personal contact, private reflection, and communion with our Creator do not appear able to compete with these examples of technology. It is indeed true that how one spends their money and time is an accurate indicator on where they place their value and worth.

However, there are many more examples of how these circumstances unfold and have deluded our walk with God.

The reality of this lack of time spent in communion with our Creator follows the idea that we need to have distractions. This affords us the opportunity to avoid facing the reality of our lives. We engage in the basic, functional activities of life to include eating, sleeping, and working. We expend varying amounts of time with our families while using the remainder of our lives to experience diversions that allow for avoidance of our circumstance. This seems to be a harsh assessment yet, one seems to avoid considering the significance associated with ensuring our eternal existence. The exercise of diversion is a definite detriment to our best interests of securing a favorable home with our Creator when we don't demonstrate the efforts necessary to secure our future. The true test to determine whether one is adequately involved in repose with God is to ask the question, "Do I talk to God when I don't need something or have a drama or active distress going on"? If one can positively state that they do spend a good deal of time in communion, separate immediate needs, they can feel good about their walk with their Creator. Understand that we all face challenges in demonstrating obedience to his expectations yet, we are well received as long as we continue to make sincere efforts at compliance. Otherwise, problems are present within the relationship.

In order to avoid any confusion for the reader as to the way in which the average individual's relationship appears to this writer. It is primarily based on what I observe to be man totally focused on humanity, (instead of) man focused on God. I qualify with this explanation. Since the 1960's and going forward the average individual spends time absent the workplace with their families and friends. The chief activities involved entertainment such as sports, music, film, media, sex, intoxicants, etc. and in each of these instances it is primarily a relationship of the person involved totally with others of the species. This is in direct conflict with an earlier time when people used their time for the purpose of development of a relationship with the Father and the Son (bible reading, church attendance, and deep, logical-deductive reasoned discussions that had a tendency to eventually turn to a consideration of the Creator by the people in conversation). This does not represent the primary way personal time is spent in the present for most I submit. I believe that a great many people do not find their conversations including our Father and the Son. Most available personal time has become centered on humanity and "man's" world for a preponderance of the population in normal situations. And this is the reason for my assertion of a lack of an adequate relationship between man and God and represents a new reality of man having an interest in self and other humans; rather than as was the previously more practical means when it was considered "God's world". This is also reflected in the present-day attendance in situations that are related to the development of that relationship.

I have heard that the percentage of individuals who attend church is somewhere around 20% with a 5% margin of error. This does not speak well for us as a nation that says that it is a Christian nation. I also witnessed how we flooded the churches the weekend after 9/11 but, within a month of that event, things returned to little participation in religious services. I believe that this number would be even less if one considered the "2fers" Christians (Easter and Christmas attendance only per year). Where did God go wrong? In reality, he didn't. Actually, a better question is when did we not continue to place God first? God has always been there for us, we just fail to take advantage of his many blessings when it requires a contribution on our parts. We fail to show participation that honors and acknowledges the omnipotence of God in our lives with time spent in communal worship. Understanding that church attendance does not guarantee salvation, it does aid in the development of knowledge associated with the traditions and ideas for a personal, spiritual relationship with God (and Son).

When there is tragedy many people blame God. The typical question is to ask, "How can a loving God allow bad things to happen"? That seems to be the way in which they avoid weighing the effects of free will and accepting that God is infinitely wiser and more loving than can be understood. Instead, it is argued that he is doing something wrong and he really doesn't love us. It does not seem fathomable to accept such horrific events without questioning God, yet a better exercise would be to assess how the actions of society have led to the potential and realization of some of these obscene acts of violence and hostility. There are indeed times when answers are not available. In the instance of the loss of life or tragic illness, we will never know why until the time that we face our Creator. There are just, in some cases, mysteries that we must overcome with faith.

The greatest challenge facing us as a nation as well as individuals is the erosion of faith. We have experienced a loss of faith in our neighbor, our family, and our country. Some also have a lack of faith in our Creator. We have reached a point where we do not believe that things will be okay. It appears reasonable to consider that things will continue to spiral downward. Our elected leaders don't appear competent to deal with the issues facing us. In our communities we don't know our neighbors as was common in earlier times. Often times our family may be fragmented with various interests apart from closing ranks as a unit. The national psyche acts as if God is irrelevant based on determining our rules for life to be off the table for relevance to his design. It is accurate submit that many individuals who have lost their spiritual soul believe that all that remains is trying to feel good. I don't really know if a large segment of the population understands the degree of love and care that our Creator has for us. They don't seem to be able to fathom how someone can love them to a degree that makes them uncomfortable and confused. I honestly acknowledge that a lot of individuals get very uneasy with the mere mention of Christ and bail out of any discussion of his sacrifices for our salvation.

The common, present-day consensus is that if someone loves you they give you things. It seems that modern humankind awaits a gift or other tangible means of the expression of that love. It is lost to the minds of most people that God loves us enough to allow us to grope and reach out, try and fail, succeed, go forward, etc. until such time as we come to realize that none of those activities can be as meaningful as the relationship one gains from obedience to God. The fact that we continue to inhabit the planet and have our needs met is ample proof of his love. There should be no substantive "gift" required. Unfortunately, many do not see that his continued patience with our behavior, ongoing provision of bounty from our earth, and unending demonstration of the earth's natural beauty as being enough. Rather, his creation acts with the mindset that it is usually more often about things to provide a temporal satisfaction, and not about the spirit.

It really is about the spirit though. The peace that is present with our Creator is that the prize that awaits us is beyond anything that we may be able to comprehend. This future date which is referred to as eternity, most can't fully realize. Imagine just how magnificent it is to be able to provide a place of repose for an unending period of time as a "gift" for obedience and subservience. There can be no comparison with any other thing provided which even remotely approximates the comprehensive nature of such a "gift". Within the consideration of this singular factor one can only marvel at the omnipotence of our Creator and of his unequaled ability to provide. This alone would be sufficient grounds to acknowledge God as all powerful, wonderful, and as the ultimate provider. When we are despondent about the state of the world, he gives us cause for celebration.

We, as human beings, place great fanfare on the development of any invention and claim that the individual responsible is somehow highly-intelligent and accomplished. If we can provide such accolades on this individual, then, how much more should we place on our Creator who has developed everything in the universe? Just one aspect of thing would be enough to be applauded based upon how we behave towards new inventions. Why then aren't we completely stupefied and awe-struck by the glory of our Creator. It seems that we have taken for granted all of the marvelous ways and means in which our universe, environment, and down to the very cellular structure operates and functions. There are not sufficient words or superlatives to accurately or consummately describe the wonder of our Creator. Yet, we are more occupied over the invention of the computer or telephone than acknowledging that our Creator made things from sheer nothingness. Whereas our inventions are based on supplies, ingredients, and compounds originating with God, he accomplished all from nothingness. We marvel at those who use his creations to invent things. These things cannot begin to compare with God.

Consider this. There have been tens of billions of people who have lived on the planet throughout the recorded and unrecorded history. The entire collection of thoughts, ideas, plans, inventions, and devices that man can possibly consider have not begun to be adequately explored. However, God knows the total collection of the thought content that can ever occur in all of time from even the beginning. He has determined all other realities that we have not even considered after the thousands of years of the planet. And, he did it in 7 days. Now I don't know what constituted a day from the biblical references; was it a literal day or was it a period of time that is in excess of this finite time limitation. Regardless, we can't even begin to fathom his intellect much less his knowledge base. I believe that we fail to fully appreciate the omnipotence of the Creator. We are not capable, it is beyond our ability to comprehend and define.

Another example worthy of considerations is that we are the product of ions of time whereby our ancestors were allowed to exist, survive, procreate, and secure the future of off-springs. This process has led to our being present on earth. At any time with millions of possible problems within the lifetime of each and every ancestor things could have gone wrong. As a result from positively address these problems, we are here. Reality is that the problems were resolved and we are the proof of this continuity to our family lineage. It is not within any percentage of probability that God doesn't exist. His supreme control allowed for each potential contingency to be navigated over the various centuries to be accounted for our existence. Further, his foresight to see many centuries within the same lens is uncanny and consummate with an intellect that is not within our potential to understand. The next time that you consider yourself also consider the unending series of events that occurred so that you exist. You can spend a lifetime and not fully appreciate the sheer improbability that you would be born without the Creator's hand.

In each of the instances presented, as well as in the instances that we can only imagine, it comes down to having the intellect to approach an understanding of his majesty. Failure to consider, or have not the ability to ponder, can be traced to ignorance of reality associated with what is important to our survival. Scripture states that more people will be lost without salvation due to ignorance. This is indeed sad and inexcusable in most instances. Mental defect is not routinely present and we were given the gift of understanding. God has equipped each of us with the ability to reason and deduce what is to our benefit. We are able to know both for the present, as well as for the future, what matters. We are asked to consider our best interests and this does not seem too inappropriate-and then act accordingly. Can it be in anyone's best interest to fail to realize that what God states as fact is indeed the way it is? Further, how can we refuse to secure their future? Unless we cannot see beyond the present moment and deny their tendency for immediate gratification, they will be lost. "Being in the moment", at the expense of considering the infinity of eternity, does not seem to be a very good tradeoff.

There is an answer to this question that is covered in scripture as well. Paraphrased the statement that basically says that, in the last days the wise will become foolish, and the foolish will become wise. In spite of all of the information and knowledge in the world today, those of much education feel that they can resolve their lives and promote their own best interests separate of their source-God. This is not to say that all people who achieve academic or financial success abandon God. However, statistics that I have seen evidence that this is a consistent outcome with the attainment of education for many professionals. It is also common for those in possession of significant material comfort. Further, scripture clearly states that in the end times there will be attempts to, ever seek knowledge, but never come to the truth. Those who are in need and dependent on things outside their control without the means to be self-reliant are more apt to understand that their source must be acknowledged as omnipotent. This paradigm is the central fact facing whether someone will, in many instances, put God first or deny his authority. Man's preference for self, science, a lack of humility to realize his fragile lacking will undoubtedly lead to his undoing if he continues his self-absorbed behaviors. Commonly, God's words are twisted to suit their ambitions and warped sense of reality based upon science that is open to revision repeatedly. I continually have seen during my time on the planet when new research has reworked earlier held beliefs concerning our world. Science is not fool proof, and in spite of their conceit for this man-made effort to understand the world, it never will be able to give ultimate truth. In fact, as science is of human origins it serves to ensure an undeniable functional imperfection. God can only be first. The sum experience of civilization denies any other conclusion. One needs only the faith of a mustard seed to fully realize that reality, based on God, is eternal.

Chapter Eight

What Is A Spiritual Life?

Traits, Principles, and Values

I do not claim to have a monopoly on this topic. Nor do I see my offering on the subject as the final word. It is important to consider that everyone must arrive at a relationship with their Creator in a way that is both satisfying and fulfilling for them. Meeting the obligation to be the servant and accept his direction cannot be ignored. This is at the beginning of even attempting to engage in a meaningful interpersonal experience with God. If we are not accepting of the roles of self in relation to God, we can by no standard responsibly engage in such an intimate relationship. He is in charge and let there be no argument about this. Equally, we must be in compliance with what he has stated at the parameters of living and guidelines for behavior. If not, we are in rebellion and we risk becoming outside of his protection due to our ongoing insolence. As we are dependent on his bounty and grace it seems sensible to attempt to be observant of his preferences and endeavor to acknowledge them. There are many principles, concepts, and ideals that I suggest that he holds dear and expects adherence to. They include:

We must practice love in our every action and as a cornerstone to our very being-

Scripture reports that Christ required that two things be accomplished, at minimum, to have fulfilled the law to be accepted for the kingdom of heaven. These obligations were to love God with all our heart, mind, and soul and to love our neighbors as we love ourselves. It really does not get much simpler than that; likewise, it cannot be more complicated as well. On the surface we must behave in all of our earthly dealings based on these ideals. It becomes difficult when the person is disagreeable, difficult, or downright belligerent. I have been told that we are to love the person and hate the sin yet it appears that sometimes the sin is the identifying feature of the person. What it boils down to as best I can tell is that God knows our hearts and sees us beneath the veneer of society and tradition, rules, and pretense. What we really believe deep down is apparent to him and we can't hide our true motivations to him. He sees our worth dependent on how we are at our deepest levels. After all, how many times have we all seen phony attempts to be gracious that were later realized as hypocritical? In the privacy of conversations away from the public a clearer picture emerges of how the person actually behaves. What we do in private goes a long way to identify who we are in reality. The love for God and for the created is something that must be continually cultivated in response to challenges of society and the temptations of the ungodly.

Honesty is always the best policy

Whereas I didn't see a specific, individual commandment concerning lying, it goes without saying that one lie is never the end to the experience. Often another one and still others are required to cover up the initial falsehood. It gets to a point when we would not even know what is the truth (and what is a lie) after repeating the falsehood repeatedly. Sometimes it has been said to me that in the interest of sparing someone's feelings, it is OK to tell a fib. This reminds me of the childhood story concerning the king's clothes. The suggestion, or moral, to the story was that an initial honesty would have saved a great deal of future embarrassment for the king. It is the childish truth of the innocents; the naïve honesty of the child, that we need to emulate. It has been stated that this is the manner in which we are to approach our salvation and our Lord. Entire lives have been puffed up with lies that fall like a house of cards when put to the test of reality by others. We are indeed doing others a disservice by allowing them to live in a less than realistic self-concept that a lie support and allow to exist. When, at some point in their lives, the lies will ultimately come out. The damage is far worse than they would have initially experienced if we had been honest with a response they do not want, yet needed, to hear.

Always put out our best effort and don't be afraid to ask God for help-

There will come a time after our last breath on Earth that we must give an accounting for ourselves. It is inevitable. We must answer for what we did with the gifts that our Creator has endowed us with. Did we work if we were able and did we contribute to the enrichment of others lives? Did we invest our skills to reap a harvest for ourselves, our family, our community, and honor our Creator? Or, did we cling to our every advantage without sharing and helping others? It is very disheartening to try hard to accomplish something and experience failure. It is even more disheartening to come to the realization that we would have been successful if we had tried a little harder (or longer). It is joyful to our Creator if we humbly ask for his help, blessings, and guidance in prayer.

As a child of the Creator it only seems natural to depend upon him for our sustenance when we are unable to do so ourselves. As practically any person who has raised children will tell you, they would not withhold any good thing from their children unless they thought that they didn't deserve it, weren't ready for it, or that it would cause them harm. Otherwise, it is relatively obvious that we should assume that we will have our needs fulfilled in the way that God believes is appropriate. Further, it will happen in God's time, and not our own. A response I have always provided in answer to spiritual concerns regarding unanswered requests of God is that it is reasonable to assume that our Creator is putting us in a position of being dependent upon him so that he can draw us closer to him. Further, a personally experienced insight as it related to my concern was God will not give me anything that will take me away from him. Even though we believe that we just "have" to have something does not mean we really do. It bares consideration of his infinite wisdom, rather than our own needs.

Don't be afraid to laugh at ourselves and don't take yourself too seriously-

Our real challenge in this life is to win the prize of eternal life which is dependent on placing things in perspective. I heard a religious leader say that God looks at our successes whereas we concentrate on our failures; without taking into account that we are human and born to labor and fail. My guiding explanation for success and achieving the prize is that we will succeed in accordance with how much we continue to stand back up. Those that are successful are those who got up one more time than they fell down. We must continue to labor and realize that we cannot build a lifetime reputation on a singular incident or moment in time. We must laugh, when we realize our actually folly. And, if you are anything like me, you will spend a great deal of time laughing at yourself.

I learned a valuable lesson concerning the reality that we are truly constantly growing without being complete. I also learned that we are not to take ourselves too seriously when I came to work at a community mental health facility as a newly graduated, supervised psychologist. I wanted everyone to acknowledge me as "doctor" with the attitude that I was truly accomplished having achieved a doctorate of psychology. It does not seem too unreasonable to acknowledge that a significant amount of effort had been personally expended to attain this title. However, I garnered a degree of resistance over time from others who saw me as practicing what was to them an uppity nature which I resented. I did not understand at that time why things were not more smoothly transpiring in my journey towards licensure. The end result was that I came to realize (finally) that the adage that to those that much is given, much is expected also included me. I needed to understand that being a doctor meant providing for the needs of others and not having relationships being primarily centered on me or my accomplishments. In reality it is not about me to any degree. Beyond the fact that I had used the talents provide by my Creator and strove to develop them, more is actually to be involved and considered. Besides, any educational certificate or degree is of man and not of God. Besides the application of this training to help others, the pride in it is not justified when considering what is important to our Creator. Reality is, education can be a point of separation from the Creator unless he gets the credit for the attainment, if is used to help others, and we deny the tendency to see it as an excuse for entitlement.

It is really all about faith and accepting that what you ask for will happen; in God's time and not our own-

What would you think if you told someone that you were going to do something and they continued to doubt you? It would be tempting to not do what you had intended to accomplish. I can see a parallel with God and his people in this respect. We have scripture that says that we ask and will receive and that no good thing will be denied to those who diligently seek him, but we ask for things then are disbelieving that they will happen. It is a question of faith and few people truly demonstrate total faith anymore. There is always a degree of disbelief or doubt and people who say that they believe in God, yet fail to accept his ability to handle our minor difficulties (in his eyes they are truly minor when you consider he created the universe). If need to accept that our troubles are but a thought away from being solved according to the principle that if we ask that mountain to be removed then it would (according to Jesus). Then we would not have to labor with a lack of faith. I perceive that our general disbelief is a source of pain to our Creator and I do not wish to contribute to his suffering. The huge issue here is that we cannot marry science and faith and we are led by science and humanistic ideals in the present age where faith has been discarded as being unable to account for our problems. Remember, science makes use of what is available to invent things or develop explanations as to the reasons and origins of our environment, God made something from nothing and did not have the availability of anyone else's contributions or assistance.

Old fashion is not a dirty word; traditional values are still relevant in today's society-

Some of the initial lessons that I learned in the first years of my elementary education and at home were about fair play and not cheating, honesty and truthfulness, hard work, personal responsibility, respect for others including our elders, and going out of our way to help others (especially the less fortunate). It was not wise to make fun of others because it is bad karma. These things have not changed although many present-day individuals don't appear to share these ideals. Everyone is looking for an advantage with the government placing them in a special class not held to the same expectations and obligations as their fellow citizens. In that respect I can speak to every group of people in one fashion or another. It includes every racial divide, both genders, and age is included as a qualifier for privilege or special status. These identifications, per our government, allow for an undeserved advantage by present political theory and operation.

The reality is that we are all in life together and when we arrive at understanding that no one should be treated "special". Instead, we are all just another citizen with equal opportunity and obligations. Only then we will be on track to come together and live out the dream of a great civil rights leader of my youth. His dream required our measurement to be "by the content of character", rather than special considerations. There is nothing wrong about being down trodden as most everyone has had this experience at some time. Accepting this place in society and expecting this status to allow for special consideration is not acceptable. We are each responsible to both ourselves (and others) to do our best and not be a burden to others who are attempting to meet their own needs. Those who work should be respected rather than expected to give an unwarranted sacrifice of their earnings and fruit of their labors for tax revenue to be given for others who claim an entitlement.

Additionally, old fashioned means (to me) applying those values in my life from that earlier age and include modesty and being humble. As an adolescent I came to understand that our bodies were not a source of promotion or to be exposed to others extensively. We were expected to be modest and dress in a manner that was a representation of the garments we wore. Pants were designed to cover the buttocks area and, with belt loops, the idea is that one wears a belt to ensure that the trousers don't fall below one's waist. This is not even considered appropriate by some presently. They suggest by their behavior a personal belief that they can expose them self with a general lack of civility regarding dress. Additionally, a sports cap has a bill on the hat for a specific, considered reason. It was done so that the wearer could shade their eyes from the sun. Now it is sideways, on backwards, etc. Generally, what I observe is a lack of simple use of common sense in these instances, and other ones like this.

In order to afford us the opportunity to consider the value of being humble, only consider the behavior of our Creator for example. He was asked by Moses who he was. Rather than be expansive and refer to a resume that includes the development of the cosmos and of everything that is within, he simply stated that "I am that I am". If there was ever anyone who had a right to be able to report anything truly extraordinary then it would be God. Instead, he was clear, concise, simply and direct as well as being unpretentious, not conceited, and humble. I believe that this expression of humble self-assessing is what is in our best interest on both the planet, as well as when called on to answer for any self-promotions at the time of being weighted by our source.

Don't make excuses and don't blame others for our failures-

People make mistakes and somehow this has become a topic to be avoided in present-day society. Every mistake is the origin for a lawsuit and no one wants to just accept that we are human and that mistakes are inevitable. When, on the other hand we are the one making the mistake, it is more fashionable to make an excuse or provide an explanation to account for this failure or problem. When this doesn't work the natural follow up is to blame someone else for the problem. This appears to be avoidance of personal responsibility as well as a lack of maturity and backbone. It is not a sin to screw up. It is a sin to place the blame where it does not belong to avoid an embarrassing failure. Personal reflection that allows us to come to grips with our own failures and shortcomings, while humbling us, is a spiritual growth experience. God cannot use us unless we are fundamentally humble and unpretentious. We must first deny our own greatness in order to be brought to the head of the table for the feast based on God's impressions of us. Not our own insight. The generally narcissistic approach to life that is presently in vogue represents a serious constriction on understanding this concept and is but one additional example of where we are straying from our origins.

To make the point more pertinent one only needs to consider the present political climate. At our federal level, within the political system it is common to hear, essentially, how our current problems are someone else's fault. The identified guilty parties may not even a part of the present government operation. Further, the cause of the distress is commonly traced to something that someone of the other party did. Consistently, it occurred as much as 20 ago or longer. This is a totally illogical and brainless exercise that does nothing to productively address the current state of confusion. Instead of blaming the prior president or the senator who has retired try to, instead, provide a means of dealing effectively with what is destroying us to benefit all of the people. It really does not matter who got us here, it is essentially more vital to quit making excuses and blaming others.

When I was growing up, my parents wanted us to act like adults and work together to deal with life. Without regard to the party affiliation try to benefit everyone based on the immediacy of the need to get it right so as to survive. This is instead of being motivated to work primarily to serve the local voters who are more concerned about a pet project for their own interests only. In reality, what I presently see reminds me of what I experienced in the third grade as we argued over the batting order of the chosen-up sides for the recess, baseball game. By the time we actually settled the issues of who get to bat first and who would be on each team over half of the recess period was over. Meanwhile, most did not even get a chance to have a turn batting due to simply failing to act responsibly, arguing, and making excuses. The common tendency to have personal favorites resulted in someone ending up being hurt, emotionally.

Say what you mean and mean what you say-be clear and to the point-

All too often there are disagreements and conflicts (both individually and as nations) because we just didn't speak plainly and say what we think. This insanity with being "politically correct" is exasperating in its' negative effect. The real discourse needed requires being genuine and authentic in our behavior. I can't begin to fathom how so many words can be uttered by someone without anything actually being said. It is a sheer exercise in idiocy to waste the time and energy of others by engaging them in discussions that have no substance, are not going in any specific direction, and do not suggest the existence of any important purpose. I sincerely believe that those who promote "political correctness" may not actually have any insight particularly useful. Although there is little of merit to share, the need to be seen and considered promotes this behavior. If they are not catered to then they need to engage others into acknowledgements their self-assessed value thru extensive, babbling essentially absent substance. If you have something of value to share with others, just spit it out and get to the point. They will decide if what is said is of value to their situation. No excessive amount of style of expression will lend any additional value to it. Remember, communication is made up of a sender, a message, and a receiver. No particular, singular word choice should divert the sender and receiver from actually dealing with the content of the message. Otherwise, there is a failure to accomplish anything of worth. As one word does not a message make, strive to understood the full expression rather than demonstrate compulsions for a part rather than the whole.

Everybody has problems but they do not represent a rationale to deny others what we have promised them that we will do for them-

One of the most aggravating things that I have to deal with in my life, and increasingly apparent with each new generation, is excuses being provided rather than output. The people that I have dealt with suggest, by their actions, that their personal problems are a basis to allow them to be unreliable. I don't need excuses, I want results. My personal problems don't provide me a basis to avoid my obligations to others. If I promise someone that I will do something for them, then I do just as I have said rather than waste valuable time engaging in weak efforts to justify myself. How my problems can excuse me from being as good as my word doesn't seem logical to assume. Perceptually, I believe that a large part of our newest generations suggest, by their actions, that they are unique and special. This is the general assumption that is suggested by their use of excuses relating to their personal difficulties to justify incompetence. It is important that they realize that, if they can't be counted on to be as good as their word, then they are just unreliable and not worthy of my time. If someone is not as good as their word based on the performance which supports their promises, then it is problematic. Unfortunately, this has become a common behavior with many and is deplorable while antagonizing others who are making efforts to get things done. A central premise our earlier history was that a person's word was their reputation. Once it was seen that their word had no value, their reputation was effectively compromised socially.

Don't expect others to do any more than we are willing to do ourselves

There are many applications to this general rule, however two come to mind. On the one hand, we have no right to expect others to provide for our needs when we don't do so ourselves. The definition of parasite is someone who depends on a host for their existence. A parasite is of no use to itself or others unless others take responsibility for its existence. In short, spiritually speaking, they are of no utility and will be pulled up from the ground and thrown into the fire as a tree that bears bad fruit. The second application that I see in this rule is that we have no right to expects others to live up to standards and ideals that we will not be willing to embrace ourselves. How can we place constraints on others when we are unwilling to put ourselves under the same limitations? It seems somewhat hypocritical to expect more from others than we are willing to do ourselves. It appears unreasonable to expect others to carry the load while we walk alongside.

This belief has taken root and represents the source of present-day dependency on government to provide for the needs of the citizen rather than the citizen providing the means for the government. Our governing instrument states that government is to provide for the "common defense, the general welfare, and the blessings of liberty" to all of its citizens. This does not allow for an interpretation of government obligations to be for "the needs of a select few who are loud in their self-declaring of their entitled status". As a lad our president asked that we, "ask not what your country can do for you, ask what you can do for your country". Present reality is that his words now ring hollowly. Ever frequently, self-interest describes societal beliefs. The result will be that we all pay a price that we cannot even presently fully realize the complete extent of.

Every time we find ourselves judging others behaviors pause, and consider whether we have committed similar transgressions (or even worse ones). Focus inwardly rather than on others. (The 5-minute rule is my definition.)

This rule seems rather simple and self explanatory. I find it useful to look at my own sinful nature when I become too self-righteous and begin fuming over others ill-will and transgressions. Things get put in the proper perspective when accepting that I am no better than other people. In some instances, I may be even more at fault than others. Remember, we will be judged by what we have done and to the same extent we have judged others. What we have done ourselves will be amplified in multiples based upon the standards we employ to others. The rule to be considered as our means of behaving is that there is only one judge and it is not me. I have enough to take care of regarding my own conduct and need to avoid causing anger from my Creator by being hypocritical. I don't have time to consider the faults of others, much less condemn them. I must consider my conduct as that is what I am to be judged for, not others behavior.

Fear the Lord as the basis of the beginning of knowledge

An often advertised vehicle rear window placard states that the individual inside does not fear anyone. The scriptural inference on the topic of fear states that by having a fear of God results in the advent of knowledge. Stated another way, it serves as the beginning of the development of intelligence. Obviously, the opposite of having a fear of God is having no fear of God. This leads to the opposite of intelligence and implies that it is the basis for ignorance and a lack of knowledge. So when those of us promote a "fear no one mentality" they are, in fact, professing their ignorance based on the idea that a lack of a healthy fear of God is consummate with ignorance of the basis of life. Fear plays a vital part of life and this attempt by society to avoid the exercise of fear of our environment is harmful to the species.

Fear ensures that we do not attempt things that would lead to harm for ourselves. Holding one's tongue rather than speaking ill of others is preferred in order to avoid receiving violence for our lack of respect or restraint versus our fellow citizen. Instead, at present it is fashionable to vent our displeasure at others who offend us without any regard for our self-preservation. Somehow, there is no mature consideration for our safety as it is deemed inappropriate for someone to allow their personal offense towards others ill-manners to cause a physical response. Somehow it is just ok to spout off at others rather than center on our own shortcomings. Instead they criticize others to keep the heat off of their own poor conduct.

Fear is at the center of restraint. Just ask a child who has received corporal punishment from their parent in the past. They are hesitant to engage in a repeat of the activity that caused the receipt of that previous punishment. Fear can therefore be said to be a result of behavioral modification. Further evidence suggests that a person will attempt to avoid repeating a previous illegal behavior due to the experienced results. They typically defer from a repeat performance. However, there is currently little ramification for poor behavior and a general lack of personal responsibility in present-day society. The development of fear is hindered much to the detriment of present generations. This lack of fear terminally affects our exercised skill at survival as we don't exhibit the minimal levels of caution which may ensure the survival of our species. It is my concern that an ill-advised launch of weapons may bring the human occupation of the planet to an end. In this instance, fear would be useful. Some actually believe that dying, while killing others in the process, is the answer to advancing their religion beliefs. Meanwhile, the liberal-left defends the right to advance these beliefs while denying the consideration of a religion that professes love as the chief aim. In this instance it constitutes an assault on civil liberties to expect favorable support.

Prison overcrowding is eased by plea-bargaining away the majority of the deserved sentence. This occurs due to dismissing many of the charges, prior to trial, because of concerns over the costs of extended incarcerations. This allows the transgressor the ability to avoid paying the full price for their transgressions. With the spending of taxes being as they are, I don't understand that spending becomes an issue in the instance of public safety. Discipline is infrequent and poorly administered to children due to parents fears of having their 6 year old turn them in at school. This seems so obscene to have a world where the child controls the parent as a result of our more enlightened liberal society. The result is that they do not develop with any restraint which results in the typical ill-mannerly behaviors. Those who frequent public places face instances when they cannot enjoy their experience due to this lack of restraint and self-control of the other's younger family members. Education suffers because the children are under no obligation to restrain themselves and feel that a good faith effort to learn is a concern. There is no fear of repercussions for poor behavior, so no immediacy to behave. In close to this address, a lack of fear is at the basis of much ill-mannerly behavior and disrespectful personage. This contributes to the developmental lack of a spiritual nature that respects the sovereignty of the Creator. Due to this present lack of fear, the obligation to be subservient in our behavior out of respect for him has been secularly voided.

Pay cash and live within your means so that you can appreciate what you have and recognize from where it came-

Since the advent of the credit card and revolving credit account many Americans, just like their governments, do not know what it means to live within their means. This fact means that they succumb to purchases that are ill–advised, knee-jerk responses they later regret. The source of much financial pain results as they must suffer in the future because of poor decisions for the purchase of things that they could have done without. Their potential manic behavior leads to less than total advance consideration prior to spending funds that they are ill-equipped to repay. This is due to possessing limited available resources or using these resources to repay while suffering due to doing without as we honor our obligations caused by our spending errors. So how is this situation associated with spirituality?

The use of credit as a means of purchase lends itself to the development of a spirit that is unable to associate personal effort with being able to own. It is less likely to be appreciative of what they own as it is not directly tied to sweat equity. Yes, you work to pay your credit card purchases but there is not a clear association with work and ownership many years later for something that is now broken or worn out. Without having expended work-related effort that culminated with a paycheck and timely purchase, the connection of this process is difficult to completely appreciate. It is reasonable to attach less gratitude to credit purchases that do not conform to the limited time-constrained attention span skills of humans for reasoning the connection between effort and reward. Ultimately, an inability to make a connection between work, ownership, and God's provision that made it all happen results. It may appear to be a stretch to follow this reasoning but only consider that we tend to have thanksgiving for what God has provided but when there is no work expended prior to ownership, there is often a lack of real gratitude as we have merely acquired another "thing" in order to be temporarily content.

Every time someone passes gas it does not require an analysis or assessment to infer the existence of a problem- chill out:

As I have already alluded to, if it doesn't matter down the road then don't make or perpetuate drama to upset yourself and others. Why make the day less enjoyable than God intended for it to be? I continually see, as the problems continues to be more acutely felt by society, that people tend to analyze everything that others do and present with a critical view of others. The extent to which criticism is practiced in social exchange was never intended by our Creator. In doing so, it appears that the strategy is to keep the heat off of them self. They don't have to feel like they are on the hot seat and forced to answer for their own shortcomings. We are to help each other weather the storm, deal with problems together, and make it beyond the issues that occur daily. Commentaries or microscopic pricking of every minute defect associated with someone or something is not intrinsically helpful to resolve the issues. We are not above examination and in order to avoid any undue and unwarranted attention to our own poor behavior, we need to lay off complaining about, speaking ill of, or belittling others. Murmuring is not complimentary or flattering and speaks ill of us by suggesting that we may be ungrateful or just miserable people.

A case in point concerning murmuring which I believe to be particularly annoying is the attitude that many have about overcast, rainy day. There is an invariable complaint about the day being "messy" or "yucky". Additional comments consider how the day is dreary or wasted due to the conditions. Consider this, would you prefer to be 6 foot under the ground or be allowed to enjoy the day. If you asked someone who was deceased if they would be alright with living an additional day if they were willing to accept the day as being rainy or overcast, I do not believe that they would turn it down. Further, everything that God has made has a value and a utility; being ungrateful while failing to appreciate his genius is a sin. Even the waste products of the organism frequently serve a useful purpose of fertilizing a plant in order for it to produce a harvest that will give us the necessary food to live and function effectively. So why do we grumble? I am totally baffled.

The afore mentioned principles associated with humility, patience, honesty, gratitude, personal responsibility, intimacy with our Creator, hard work, financial restraint, conservatism, as well as a fear of, faith in, and relationship with God are at the cornerstone of the development of a spiritually-sound existence. Having a grateful heart and peace-filled countenance is also necessary. These trait factors have been forwarded for much of the American experience. They represent a primary reason for our success of the country. Unfortunately, they are not readily practiced or honored by a sizeable number of Americans. This could ultimately lead to a great loss for our future prosperity. These principles may appear old-fashioned and out-of-step with the "modern America" but they, nevertheless, are at the bedrock of success for much or our heritage. Many who have been practiced these traits will attest to their value and virtue.

Finally, our on-going responsibility, absent these mentioned traits and values that is most fundamentally to the understood as our duty to others must be considered. We are, not only to pray for others, but take actual everyday actions to ensure that we live out the responsibility to be our brother's keeper. As such we must, as our testimony to our faith to and love of God and the Son acknowledge:

The most fundamental obligation, as well as a basis for our personal hope of acceptance by our source is based on our obligation to continually attempt to reach others to assist them in an understanding of their need to be obedient to, and develop their own relationship with, their Creator.

If we wish to have our God provide ongoing consideration for acceptance after leaving earth, we must provide the same ongoing credit and consideration to everyone else during our lives. If we don't, we run the risk of having God, in effect, decide to give up on us just as we do on others. As frustrating as it is to share the "good news" and be rejected, there are those who believe that they only need to consider their salvation once they have been informed of their impending demise due to a terminal illness. In other instances, they may be denied the time to consider due to a quick, unexpected death. I question the ease of forgiveness if one operates based on that belief system. I am curious as to the motives behind the attempts to curry favor with God at that point. However, as only God knows our hearts, it is his decision as to the sincerity of which the forgiveness is asked for. From a practical standpoint, we are all reaching out due to a faith in God as the final arbitrator (as well as because of a fear of the unknown). However, as

Jesus taught in the parable of the workers, people can be saved even at the end of their lives, so. This being so, we cannot dispute that salvation is always possible due to the infinite love of our Creator for us, his creation (in spite of the human suspicions that I just considered). As true servants we are to do the master's work, therefore, always advance his cause of bringing home every possible person to the flock. There is no justification to operate as if we are in any way an authority regarding who was worthy of receiving salvation. We do not know our brother's heart or of their personal relationship with our mutual Creator. Even though the work may be a test for us, never grow weary in helping each other in our journey to reach out and find our way home to God and the Son. Nothing is easy (especially planting seeds in the minds of the lost) so, have patience.

Chapter Nine

What Is Important

Living In a Secular World

In a discussion of determining what is of value and importance for the life of humans, it is useful to examine the experience of living by prioritizing the functions of life. Eating, sleeping, gathering resources for consumption and to promote self-preservation, procreating, raising off-springs to ensure the survival of the species, and banding together to consider the need for mutual survival are considered important. These considerations are an essential basis for meaningful development of the human beyond a primitive state of existence. Once we derive the satisfaction of these needs, then considering our existence follows. To continue to operate merely to satisfy the primitive functions seems senseless without a higher purpose. Science states that we have derived from members of the animal kingdom as expressed by the theory of evolution. Somehow, man and woman have always envisioned themselves as something more than that during our past civilized history. Only in the recent times has this been considered a fallacy by our secular perspective.

Another likely area of consideration that occurs, even while we struggle with survival involves asking how we got here. This leads to the acknowledgement from a spiritual-based viewpoint that it wasn't by chance. For most of recorded history the prevailing wisdom was that there was a God, or collection of gods, responsible for our existence. Within our recent past, the idea was made that we are derived from apes. Beyond this, mere chance has emerged as part of description of evolution of our specie. This idea leads into the discussion of what is important because it rather tellingly suggests that humankind's revolt against the Creator began in earnest at that point. This theory, as the initial salvo, is important and needs to be recognized as worthy of discourse. In an earlier time in history it would have quickly and accurately been stated that serving God was our duty and purpose. Being obedient and mindful of God's instructions was the essential way of playing out this purpose of life. In short, God is what was important and the counter argument by present, humanistic ideals is that man has attempted to place them self as an equal position.

Rather than just be on equal footing, God is now ignored and disavowed so that discussion of the merits of obedience are outdated. Rather than subservient position to God, I have seen research that says that in the present state of the specie, he is considered irrelevant. This represents a serious problem. Mind you, we are primarily speaking about western, secular culture that is self-absorbed with science. This is where secular, humanistic-thinking has predominated over the past 50 years and where the major themes associated with this movement has occurred. As it stands, other cultures that promote murder and violence to gain compliance to their religion are equally abhorrent to God. They represent middle-eastern, Islamic zealots who are trying to undo all of their people's efforts at participation in representative government. This being said, the sheer insanity of our world with all civilized entities participating in different ways, has placed us in what is a world that is not peaceful or sustainable.

A central loss for secular humankind is that perceptually, the lifetime here on Earth is the beginning and end of the human experience. The scriptural description of our earthly life as being described as a mere vapor is the essence of their existential reality and serves as the fundamentally important total source of value. This is without due attention to eternity or so it seems to be the inference by humanism. If there is no faith in God, instead, we are our own gods, and we alone are responsible for our future or so it seems accurate to conclude from their conduct. What does the secular person have to look forward to? Where does the secular person turn when things go wrong? When they experience a horrific event beyond their ability to process occurs, how do they respond? It never ceases to amuse me that the secular person can deny the deity of God, yet will call on him when they can't deny the reality of their insignificance. If they were in an airplane on its' way unfettered towards a crash onto the earth, I envision that reality would be that they would be pleading with God for a way out. Unfortunately, for most, they don't ask for this assistance in their life due to what I see as an arrogance that is undeserved. Too late they may be left to lament their avoidance of a relationship with the Creator (or so I suppose).

This lack of consideration and value of the hereafter results in probability of stress for the unspiritual, or marginally-spiritual. My experience is that these people are so concerned about the here-and-now, that they can't ponder the reality that most things are really not that important and won't matter within a few years from now. Their compulsive nature is to keep time fully occupied with an ongoing drama (from which stress results) and this nature has become a central feature of their lives. If one considers the next world, and what is necessary to be a party to it, they don't spend their time incessantly concerning themselves with every detail of the here-and-now. It won't matter in the long run, so why add to the drama and their stress? One is either concerned about achieving status in this world or of being found sufficient to enjoy a future time to come. So, in actuality, it comes down to immediate gratification versus being able to delay gratification. This stress-laden life has led to a state of irrationality and failure to consider remaining compliant with our Creator over misplaced importance associated with their short-term interests. The valuing of the created over the Creator has, as a side effect, a situation where the vitally important existential concept of hope is not operating. The belief in a place beyond this state of existence gives us this hope. Things will be so incredible and beyond our ability to realize the full benefit is the thought. Thus, our trials in life don't take on such an overwhelming burden to squash our joy. The end result of constantly attempting by secular methods to experiencing joy, as an artificial and non-spiritual activity, is essentially a shallow hedonism activity that is absent the deeper peace from understanding of eternity.

When speaking of how humanity has behaved, it is appropriate to state that both genders are equally in rebellion against God. Ample evidence bears this out. The mother claims a secularly codified, legal "right" to abort her off-springs during pregnancy. The result is the extermination of millions of unborn babies and this is only within the past 50+ years. Those of the liberal press present this controversy in society based on the rights of the mother rather interest in the unborn. Although significant opposition exists to this practice, the media avoids responsible attention to their concerns. Scripturally, it states that woman's lot is to bear children for their part in the debacle that occurred in the Garden of Eden. God did not provide for rights concerning childbirth, it was merely that woman would be responsible for this function to perpetuate society. This is a no nonsense interpretation that does not use secular practices such as splitting hairs or using emotional labeling to consider the issue. Since murder is a crime and the unborn is a person whose life is being involuntarily ended, then it is not permissible as a common scriptural-based commandment. God gave the instructions and admonishment-not me. My reasoning comes from this commandment and scriptural prose that states God knew us while we were in the womb. This statement leads me to infer that we are, even then, are human beings to him.

However, man contributes to this rebellion as well. It has been estimated that over 70% of the fathers of some racial groups do not take the responsibility for their off-springs. Their children are born out of wedlock with the father not providing emotional or financial support. This leaves the government taxpayers picking up the tab for the child's expenses. When God stated that woman would experience the pains of childbirth, he also proclaimed that man would toil for his survival. That toil included providing for his family. If he didn't he was "worse than an infidel". In biblical times, infidel was as abusive, profane term in line with some of our most colorful, current vulgar language.

So why is this so important? Every structure or entity is made up of building blocks that work together to form the whole. This provides the whole with the ability to function. The whole of civilization is made up of the individual building blocks and the union of man and woman make up the initial and most significant portion of the puzzle towards the continuation of the human race. We can entertain the debate of homosexual unions or "same-sex marriages" but it really doesn't, in the final analysis, merit acceptance or a judgment. The reality remains that they will die off having provided no legacy to continue the human lineage that they chose to end (or even prove evidence that they existed). It is their loss due to the lack of participation in the grand design of humankind that requires that the union of man and woman must necessarily occur. (One theory that I have read is that most individuals are fundamentally forgotten after 4 generations removed except by direct ancestors. or if considered historically significant). This is really another instance associated with the theme of the rebellion against the Creator. What is so tragic for humankind is the diminished importance placed on the marriage of man and woman. It is more common that significantly so, marriages end up in divorce. Home life absent the contributions of both gender perspectives led to juvenile delinquency and drug abuse. Legal and social service interventions are rampant and the primary contributing factor is the absence, or lack of strong, parental direction and guidance for the children due to failed marriages. This leads to even more rebellion, initially as youngsters and continuing into adulthood. The evidence of the need for parenting that, early on, sets the stage for obedience to authority-including God's, cannot be underestimated. It serves as a proximal cause to our disintegrating social fabric.

This rebellion includes an ambivalence and learned ignorance towards our previous adherence to our Creator. Now we are now in charge of our world. This attitude has much of its origins as a by-product of the age of science. We tell ourselves that we know our world and can manipulate it as its masters. We know what our world consists of, how it operates, and believe we are able to control the environment as, in effect, the manager of the universe. Having identified the basis of the conceptual identity for our existence, man believes that he has support for the opinion he "has got this". The impression that I come away from a conversation with a science-oriented theorist is that we are on par with our Creator. The subtly suggested idea is that we are now in collaboration thereby suggesting equal status. No longer is it cool to take orders or accept a subservient status.

Within the guise of science, we fail to consider that everything that science tackles must occur on some level with the use of what is available. Science cannot produce absent the availability of a preexisting element. It must use available commodities that only a God could make. In fact, this is the initial error which denies any possible suggestion of the rightness of the theory of evolution. No matter how it is stated, our existence was at some point originated by an outside entity, chance is not a beginning step. We cannot make something from nothing and this represents a crucial difference between man and God. Our present rebellious attitude ignores this elementary consideration. In spite of this, we teach our children with textbooks that highlight man's accomplishments as if to suggest that we really are that impressive. It would have been more appropriate for our students, early on, to be given the opportunity to compare (impartially) God's accomplishments with those of man through presentation in school textbooks. A more robust understanding by the student would invariably result in a higher comparative value of God over man. Due to the sad reality that this practice has existed for multiple generations in the classroom, we now irreverently consider our origins as inconsequential. Without comparative considerations for our source versus the created, society arrogantly considers self as important absent the dependence we deny.

So, what is important? To obey, consider, acknowledge, serve, love, and cherish our Creator for his gift of life to us and place him first in our every deed, thought, and action. That is the essence of what is truly important and critical to our well-being. Since our well-being is at the driving force for our actions (or should be) then it is only appropriate to believe that we are dependent upon our Creator for our benefits. His grace allows us to fall short and still continue to exist. In reality, when something is not working it is reasonable to consider changing things so that is corrected. It seems rational to consider this be appropriate. In spite of this apparent accurate consideration we keep making indiscretions and fail to be called out. Our Creator continues to labor for us in spite of our apparent rebellious examples of behavior for what seems to be an eternity.

Also, being successful in the sense of being compliant and obedient with the commandments and rules of living provided by our Creator is important. I do not believe that if God didn't have a definite opinion or didn't have expectations then he would not have given us his guide for living. I often ask my clients what they would do if they were going to repair an automobile. The usual answer is that they would depend on reading an instructive manual for assistance in order to know what to do. The fact that living life requires understanding with expectations and guidelines makes it appropriate to have a manual for that purpose as well. Life is so complex, ever changing, yet constant in its challenges that one must reflect on some guidance to successfully navigate through the problems and difficulties that present themselves to us all. The scriptures have helped people around the world for many centuries. It is not an accident that the Bible is the most popular and printed texts in the history of the planet. It was considered a great progress in society when the general public was able to get a copy due to the invention of the printing press. People have been killed over the possession of the texts in some counties. In others, the mere ownership of a few pages leads to imprisonment and torture. In western society, it is a common liberal practice to refer to those who cite the scriptures as "Bible Thumpers". The suggestion is that they are not positive members of today's culture. They are mocked and I continue to be amazed by the ignorance demonstrated by those who don't know the contents included in the text yet have sport of those who do. It only seems right to investigate something before making light of it. It seems highly disrespectful to make fun of our Creator's instructions. However, this is a signal activity of present society and I feel that it will incur a penalty for those who do not profit from it.

Practically all of the principles and beliefs that I have discussed are directly or indirectly from scripture and scripture-related ideals. It is clearly stated that we are to advance the species through procreation, know our roles within the family organization as God has defined the family rather than as secular society has diluted those roles to. We will give an accounting for our time on the planet and answer whether we produced for both ourselves and others. Did we promoting the kingdom of God? Did we love others without condition, were we meek and humble, did we work for what we want and need rather than be dependent on society, and did we have enough pride in ourselves to stand for God's principles in spite of the insults of others? I believe, acting in ignorance to God's plan while demonstrating a preference for secular, man-made guidelines will be detrimental. Because our time on earth is only temporal and our time in eternity is without end, we should be mindful of always placing God first in our lives. These things represent what is essentially important for our present and future security, both on this planet as well as in the hereafter.

Another way of expressing the need for regarding relative importance to daily lives is simple explanation that is humble but direct. If one works and supports themselves and their family, stays away from drugs, and is willing to be cordial with humility towards others then things would work out much better than it does at present. If we worked for our needs and the needs of the other important people in our lives, the government would not spend the amount that they do. Taxes would be lower and the deficit would be close to nonexistent. We would not be killing our fellow humans or imprisoning others due to drug-related crime. Drug abuse would drastically lower our prison population. We were providing for our temples (body) in a proper manner. And if we treated others the way that we wanted to be treated, violence and abuse would be practically nonexistent. Is that not important and desirable? And it all starts with the way we approach our responsibilities to ourselves and others as well as the method and means with which we live and exist. God's instructions are explicit and so relevant to this outcome that they are primary to the success (if these things were to occur).

Perhaps the single most important aspect to our being and way to positively affect others is the expression of love. Scripture says that God is love, it is imperative that we attempt to mirror that which is at the center of our spiritual existence. However, it is one of the most elusive and difficult trait factors to consistently emulate. Our humanness and tendency to consider our self as the primary source of truth causes us problems. We believe our world must be a specific way and, when it is not so, it causes us frustration and great angst that potentially serves to sabotage our relationships with everyone. It is the cause of wars between nations as well as being the chief cause for termination of many interpersonal relationships. In fact, the most difficult lessons that I have had to learn (and am still learning) is that I don't need the answers, I do not possess a monopoly on the truth, and it is not the most important thing to be right. What matters is that I love everyone and leave the judgment to God. It is entirely possible that our purpose while alive is to learn the lesson of love and to become proficient in its exercise. In spite of the fact that this seems easy, I am sure that most would admit we do not master it consistently.

There are other, less vital activities, which are important to the species. An important thing to consider is that anything that is made should have utility. In some instances it seems that the primary purpose is to view the beauty of its existence. We, as human beings, are no different and should have utility. In short, we should accomplish something of worth to account for our time on the planet and this is, to me, important. In the final analysis, we will be called upon to give this accounting of ourselves. Did we use the skills, resources, and time we were allotted by our Creator wisely? And this accounting must take account the consideration of the principle of collectivism applied to our existence. Rather than "I" or "me" it should be based on "us" as it relates to our connectedness to the world we shared with others.

We, as God's creatures, primarily consume and use what is on the planet for our enjoyment and sustenance. We must replace the resources consistently and use other resources frugally. This ensures that resources will continue to be available for succeeding generations. The problem for many is that we have evolved into a primary consideration for "me". Frequently, opinions and decisions have their origins from the standpoint of "I" rather than "we" and "us". The term "family of man" means that we are a part of something much bigger than ourselves. We must be ever mindful of the responsibility to consider others and their needs, as well as our own. This is vitally important to both our continued success, the success of others, and having the accounting of our life satisfactorily insured. I would venture to say that a significant principle of spiritual living requires placing our self after others based on the formula of God first, followed by the needs of others, and finally us. In spite of the fact that it often seems that we are going to run out of something, there always ends up being enough for us. This is in spite of the concern for fulfilling the needs of others and running out before we have our needs met. That is the beauty of God's plan for our provision. The best interests of all are equally assured and, in the end, not one of his obedient children will be left out of the Lord's feast.

Chapter Ten

Is The Entire World Going Insane?

Going to the Brink of Madness

The basic theme of the book has highlighted the many transgressions against God's blueprint. This is an ongoing, present-day rebellion as a society and civilization. In disrespect for his provision, we are contrary to his guidance while continuing to disobey him as societal policy. There can be no doubt that there will be a time when all of these aspects to our being will be dealt with by our Creator. He has been, by my estimation, tormented by our insolence without any conscious demonstration of remorse. Scriptural-based ideals have been ignored and tossed aside due to our drive to achieve a pleasurable state. This lifestyle philosophy is endorsed by many, while suppression of cultural guilt over the abandonment of God is avoided.

What pains me is making these admissions, but it is the reality of the time in which we live in. As a child my grandparents corrected me for my misadventures, yet were loving in their comments as they knew that "you meant well, and will learn to not do it (the misdeed) again". When this is the case, we can be expected to be given consideration. Present reality is that many are blatantly arrogant in their misconduct. It appears that they believe they aren't obligated to follow laws and are aggressive towards anyone who points out their behavior. In such a situation, I do not believe that our Creator will be lenient as my experience from my reflections from childhood learning experience would indicate.

I recently communicated with my mother about my effort in preparing this manuscript and remarked that it seemed that I may be a "doom and gloom type of guy". "The vast majority of the information is negative" I remarked. Her response was, "unfortunately, you are not far off from how things actually are". It seems that every generation has a challenge to address as it equates with leading a spiritual life. Or said another way, each generation strips one more sheet of veneer away from the spiritual nature of our existence as it was taught to us by scripture. Every age has taken away some truth from our modus operandi. A truism is that we continue to go further and further away from what is expected of us by God. Or, as it was characterized by a fellow mental health professional, every generation lowers the bar of perversion regarding what is considered acceptable and permissible.

To even speak of the many ways we have failed our God is to be seen as being a prude and out of step with present-day society. My values require me to be more concerned about being respectful of my Creator, than finding acceptance by man. Scripture says that we cannot serve two masters and that is true. We will love the one and hate the other. So I choose making an ongoing, conscious effort to follow my God's lead. This does not change due to whatever expense that I may be forced to pay by a world gone mad. So as not to be thought of as speaking in riddles, let me be clear. What follows is but a brief description of some rather limited examples of present-day standards that ignore God's guidance and directions as provided within scripture. Not only are they in opposition to an earlier time such as the Middle Ages, rather, these practices were considered appropriate for how one lived as close as the 1960's. This appears to be when it all began to come unraveled.

The initial misstep began over 100 years ago when creationism was debunked as a fable and we were told that we evolved from an aquatic form, to an ape, then to a human. This distorted theory served as the first evidence of the consideration for science by man as preferable to God's guidance. It also began the process of our separation from our Creator because it suggested that we were not made in our Creator's image. The personal connection between our Creator and his creation, of whom were formed by his hands and in whose lungs he breathed life to begin our existence, was disputed. Things continued to progress onward from there with no end to the theme of our being mere animals rather than creatures formed in the image of our Creator. Schools readily promote this theory and reject any mention of creationism in the classroom. Those who defended a spiritual-minded discussion of our origins were accused of violating others civil rights. It was inferred while dismissing creationism that those who had that belief were rigid, ignorant, and simple-minded individuals who did not accept man's discoveries from science as fact.

More recently, even into the 1960s, a couple became married prior to living together. It was believed that courting should occur and intimate sexual relations were reserved for a married couple. Once married, the goal of ensuring the continuation of the line as well, even earlier, of the human race, was professed as the primary rationale for a married sexual relationship. There was a time when the event of the birth of a child that ensured the continuity of the family line was a very significant event. Sex did not gain its value from a basis of experiencing personal pleasure but served to resolve a reasonable concern for continuity of humanity. Society and civilization regarding the threat of extinction absent the continuation of the species a concern. Now, sex is seen as a hedonistic pleasure rather than as necessary to continue human existence. The advances of medicine as demonstrated by present-day, safer childbirth and improved follow up, early-childhood medical care have mitigated concerns for survival of the species as immaterial. The function of sex is viewed for being a source of pleasure rather than a means of assuring survival. It seems reasonable to consider that God naturally made it pleasurable or there would have been no guarantee of the continuation of humankind. However, it remains doubtful that his concern was primarily hedonistic. Due to the hedonistic philosophy of today, even more extreme sexual practices have become acceptable. The change in society that considers pleasure rather than procreation for legitimacy of behavior has fueled legal decisions which do not find scriptural support.

With the prohibition against premarital sex lifted, the primary consideration for pleasure found additional expression with the use of drugs so that one could expand their world. Later adolescents and young adults acted based on the concept of curiosity with drug use being the new norm. Still later, mass acceptance of drugs by society has contributed to our deterioration due to legal, health, criminal justice, and mental health costs which hamper our tax base and rob our society. Not only has drug use been a scourge on society, they are responsible for the lack of inhibitions that allow criminal behavior and have clogged our court systems and fill our jails furthering the tax burden. Less time for sentencing of drug-related crimes and less interest in controlling availability of substances has been the response by society. Not only has pot become a topic of national debate for legalization, further, liberals bemoan that the prisons are primarily made up of drug-related offenses. They do not support the notion that the sale of drugs is a violent crime. This is in spite of seriously addicted people dying from overdose from the drugs sold to them by these individuals.

Within the next 10 years the previously unacceptable behavior of killing one's own innocents was refuted. Legal "overthinking" resulted in a twisted preference for secularly theorized rights over moral traditions that supported the inherent value of life. Fundamentally, the responsibility to account for the results of one's behaviors, especially when a life is involved, fell to a new standard which allow accountability to be optional. The present lack of concern for continuation of the specie has had an impact on the genesis of this controversy. Since the planet has theoretically surpassed its safe limit for population managing the number of births is considered appropriate. Failure of mass epidemics to occur in the recent history has resulted in support for abortion. Now, in a continuation to this mindset it is rational and reasonable to consider convenience as important to the decision to have a child or abort. It seems absolutely insane to me when considering scriptural principles of going forth and multiplying, to look at human life with any rational consideration being based on convenience. This idea is so insensitive to the value of the human condition that it is insulting to my sense of acknowledging the immeasurable worth of humanity.

Regarding the spiritual basis for the covenant of marriage finds both genders failing to honor their responsibilities to each other. The scriptural basis of the relationship required the man to love the woman as Christ loves his church. In return, the wife was expected to recognize the husband as the spiritual head of the home. This does not mean that this idea is not practiced in some marriages, rather, it appears infrequent in application. The common pun that I have heard is that once the two marry (and go away on their honeymoon), they will determine "who wears the pants in the family". This is inconsistent with the covenant relationship guidelines established by our source that identified marriage as the basis for our social continuation of civilization. The concern I see in working with people regards how things can be effectively managed for parenting and needs when the responsibilities are not clear. Observed conflict over control in making decisions affecting the household seem to be increasingly more common with the erosion of traditional roles and expectations. Although by present-day standards it may be considered as old-fashioned, the male is the head of the spiritual household although, judging by the lack of church attendance in America, he is failing to live up to his obligations. Now it is common to hear it said that "if momma is not happy, then no one is happy". This is, although humorous to hear, an apparent conflict with scriptural ideals concerning roles and responsibilities for family. My understanding of the spiritual basis for family life was supported by the demonstrated behaviors of my elders who studied scriptural prose routinely. I respected and obeyed my parents but the final decision was made by my father. My mother was clear in reminding me that she was not a court of appeals, his decision was final.

Although it began much earlier, the middle 70s saw the woman of the house providing a second family income. This resulted in less monitoring and guidance being provided to the off-springs during periods out of school. It is fair to say that a desire for more money trumped this previous concern to ensure the off-springs optimal development into adulthood. Sometimes out of necessity additional income was pursued, however the societal impact on individuals to "keep up with the Jones" had an undeniable effect. The pursuit of things was deemed more important due to media marketing. Due to all the things that one must have the seeds were planted in the minds of the need to consume. The result was that school systems now took on the responsibility of not only educating the child, but providing the liberal spin on life. This seemingly innocent scenario has been a highly significant factor in the secular and liberal philosophical explosion in the past 3 decades as the youths grew up and took over the business of running our world. In short, it was often a value judgment where the pursuit of money and what it could provide outweighed the obligation to train up the child in an admonition of the Lord. It bears noting that there were instances when the mother had no choice due to the lack of the availability of adequate, deserved support. However, the drive for things has had a serious negative impact and this cannot be denied. There are instances when families believe that two incomes are required to subsist. This may be due to few marketable skills such that income is not high from work.

When the father does not take on the primary responsibility inherent by biblical explanation to provide for the family, the woman has no choice but to pick up the slack. Yet, when there is conflict in the household and a drive to control by each party without reasonable compromise the home has no peace. The result may be that each parent goes it alone with a decision to separate or divorce. It is the child who ultimately suffers and, without direction and appropriate modeling, this scene continues to reoccur as each child becomes of adult. The pattern of interpersonal conflict and disappointment is a vicious cycle.

This change in the role of woman has had serious consequences for society. However, the liberal press is not satisfied with their successes at redefining the role of women in society. They have now claimed that there is a war on women as a diversion for political capital to continue control over society. This represents an insult to both women and our Creator's design for them. On the one hand, it is inferred that a man's work outside the home is more important than the raising, shaping, and training young minds. Otherwise, why would women prefer to work outside the house and compete with men for position and power? This appears to represent the demonstrated train of thought of liberal left strategist. Their attempt to destroy the sum total of the civilized experience seems to have taken on a new twist. The lessons of over 6 thousand years of civilization suggest an added importance to secure the future of the family. This ensures that society has moral, thoughtful, docile, and amicable off-springs to assure civilizations ongoing prosperity. This is much more important than a job outside of the household but this supposed "war" supports a divergent position that men's work is more important. Women naturally prefer competition for position over parenting children and supporting a family is the hypothesis. This is the latest in the ongoing insult for the expressed design from the Creator. Old fashion as the roles of mother and father appear when considering the present age, if it was good enough for the family of Christ, I do not feel certified to argue against it.

In many instances the woman may have to be a breadwinner to support the kids while the man fails to either provide any meaningful support. It is now common for taxpayers to pay for his children's needs while the father ignores his obligation to give support to his creation. In some cases, the father is not even in the house and will not marry the mother of his children so that she is eligible for welfare payments. In other instances, the failure to agree is seen as grounds to terminate the relationship while leaving the children in the lurch without parental guidance, love, or financial resources to live sufficiently to learn the lessons necessary to live productive, responsible adult lives. The overwhelming disruption from a lack of a stable family structure cannot be overlooked as a primary cause of the lack of discipline, responsibility, and morality in the present age. Divorce is at a rate that is hard to support. It isn't reasonable to assume that over 50% of marriages were affected by adultery or abuse (what God deems grounds for dissolution of vows). Instead, they were poorly-planned and based upon physical attraction without serious, mature considerations prior to entering into marriage in numerous instances. And all of society pays for these poorly considered decisions that were based on a lack of restraint and mature consideration for the responsibilities of marriage. These irresponsible behaviors that lead to illegitimate divorce are not based upon scripturally acknowledged basis for divorce. This is the senseless end to marriages witnessed by, and with vows exchanged, in the presence of God. This provides ongoing evidence to the carefree irreverence for such a special covenant that we have been blessed with by our source.

And presently, there exists a push to acknowledge "rights" for homosexuality that allow for marriages for same gender couples. The results include challenges for many Christian who consider these marriages from the standpoint of scriptural prose. Meanwhile, society expects the spiritually-led citizen to accept what is scripturally denounced. The actual behavior that lends the name to them was unacceptable in the rural, conservative community that I grew up in. It was considered immoral by common religious instruction at that time. Those who honored our God's instructions did not approve or condone this behavior. This instruction was derived from the printed biblical text that provided reoccurring examples of representation of marriage based on each gender representing the family structure. Now individuals have been sanctioned to engage in marriage that is constituted by same-sex partners due to legal decisions. These individual appear to have no qualms about the behaviors or acts associated with being a homosexual. This is compared to when I was a younger person when being identified as such was not a positive development socially.

Further, they expect others to accept this behavior and embrace their identifying behaviors as the new norm for society. Further, our government gives them sanction and attempts, through judicial decision, to legitimize a behavior that is not accepted by those who strictly observe God's scriptural prose as something that they would personally practice. What is necessary is to understand that our Creator accepts those who repent, even into the 11th hour. This suggests that individuals can, in effect, sin for the vast majority of their existence yet be accepted for salvation. It follows that they come to understand their sin and sincerely seek repentance for this to happen. I don't know if this extends to what scripture terms as an abomination? Somehow, I don't see this happening for a sizeable number who sometimes marching in the rallies to flaunt their "pride" in their homosexual behavior. Although legal by man within the laws of present-day, secular society, it is not scriptural supported. This is clear to my understanding within my reading and study of scripture that God does not approve. Reality remains he will have the final word and, ignorance or defiance, will not deter his judgment.

This new reality supporting homosexual marriages presents societal circumstances which provide instances of insult to the Creator beyond the obvious nature of the behavior. To understand the stark extent to which the insult is demonstrated, consider the disregard for the Creator that their pursuit of union sometimes includes. I have read in media print that these individuals wish to have a church wedding to cement their union. Just momentarily consider the symbolic nature of what is being asked. The church represents a place of worship that is considered as a house of God. Considering what has been ascribed to him in scripture regarding the manner of behavior in question, it seems to represent a level of irreverence beyond belief. This lack of judgment that justifies a ceremony which is in opposition to spiritual traditions is totally baffling. Certainly, it seems only appropriate to understanding the depth of the challenge to his authority that concluding this arrangement in his presence (in his "house"). The inevitably potential end results when accountability is incurred at the future point, notwithstanding the practiced behavior separate the ceremony, is to an extreme very well unimaginable. I guess that my puzzlement is similar to what my mother would ask me as a small child when she would ask me, "What were you thinking?"

Meanwhile, the schools continue to teach children ongoing liberal philosophy which includes evolution, dismissing gender roles, and promoting beliefs central to secular philosophy. Any reference to creationism and God is strictly prohibited. The schools have ensured over the past 40+ years the exclusion of the knowledge of God from the classroom thereby fulfilling expressed goals to have a world absent God. The child does not benefit from an understanding of our connection to our Creator. The principle of religious freedom and the fact that this led to the origins of development of America is, likewise, packaged with negative connotations. Our founding fathers, pioneers, and explorers that were proudly described in an earlier time are dishonored in current texts for student study. In the earlier time, these Americans were given a hallowed place as contributors to our development as a nation which, until recently, was the envy of the world.

After building and developing the country, these personalities have become villains and the country has been offered up to those who may not be able point beyond the current generation as residents of the country. Many of us are able to point to the earliest populating of the colonies as a time when our ancestors either lived or died dependent on our savvy and resource. Now, we provide every financial resource to those who enter America without any obligation for assimilating into the culture. They are not even obligated to learn the cultural symbolism (language) of this country as evidenced by dual-language practice in current business. They have not adopted our national perspectives, meanwhile we are told by the liberals that we should be ashamed of ourselves for expecting those who immigrate to the United States to contribute.

It is stated that there is no duty to country required in order to receive welfare support. It is not considered a legitimate consideration to expect them to incorporate our values and customs into their own lifestyle. In some instances, they may be in the country illegally. Liberal mindset ignores this illegal behavior and the part that breaking the law played in their being in the country. Couching the circumstances of the illegal intruders in a way that fundamentally ignores immigration law, instead, we are told we are "haters" for denying opportunity. Instead, they have approached this position as they do with all other issues; throwing money at the problem is the solution. This demonstrated lack of logical deductive, higher-level reasoning, and moral considerations regarding security of its citizens often represents liberal policy. The operating idea sees minority encroachment on our borders representing future voters if provided favor. Meanwhile, consistently practices of liberals include bad-mouthing those who believe that exerting toil and supporting through tax revenues provides a right to question the lack of respect for their interests.

Thus it can be said that every generation further erodes our relationship with our Creator. This is due to rebellion against the instructions provided for proper living and design for humankind by him. Also, our nation seems embarrassed about its heritage and apologetic to every group that presents with an axe to grind in blaming their status on others. My conservative perspective considers that one should roll up their collective sleeves to improving their lot. Wining is immature. Further, those who market race as an ongoing issue seem bent on fermenting hatred between the races. This is opposed to trying to bring us together as children of our Creator who must either work together or watch our future deteriorate to a state of chaos. And, rather than expect present-day contributions of its citizens towards a national objective, we have no goal, vision, or unifying objective. Instead, disunity and preoccupation with living in a manner that is blatantly lacking in the acknowledgement of scriptural principles is the national standard. What has been just described is a short list of present-day indiscretions yet there could be a much greater elaboration available.

The most recent assault on God includes those who aren't even accepting of their birth gender. In essence, although not directly stated the suggestions is that God made a mistake in their creation. This is the latest in an ongoing disrespect that suggests that our Creator is not perfect and we are not obligated to recognize him respectfully. The most basic and fundamental aspect of life, our identity, as well as the most personal relationship, that of our relationship to God as our Creator, is now being questioned further. It is suggested that we should actually give serious credence and legitimacy to what I perceive personally as distorted confusion over self. In short, the thinking would follow that God made a mistake or that one does not believe that he operates in our lives. Further, he is not involved or active in the unfolding story of civilization. Finally, following the idea further it results in the suggestions that God made the world then went into retirement with us left us to our own devices.

This represents a dangerous misrepresentation of scripture which states that he knew of us when we were but in the womb. We are all accounted for since the beginning of time as well as within the book of life is stated in scripture. Instead, our senses are not sufficient or appropriate to provide accurate attention. Our gender is open to a determination based on feelings rather than a visual inspection of the individual that would display organs clearing up confusion. My related ancestor, Sir John Locke, believed that we understood our environment based upon the use of our senses. Our new world refutes this idea as ineffectual. Essentially, even though we see it, it is only an illusion or so the impression is suggested. Such a seemingly illogical way of understanding our world is the new frontier of thought by scientific expression. Further, it supposes that "feelings" are the basis or reality. Humanistic theory supports someone "feels" a certain way makes it so. We are not to object since accountability is now inappropriate. (In this instance it is regarding supporting thought content). Merely an acceptance of their expressed feelings as reality is proper ettitique.

This can be disputed in many ways but I will only briefly elaborate on this idea. Thinking that we are something does not necessarily make it so. Otherwise, when one believes that they feel a certain way it must be reality according to arguments supporting recent pronouncements over identity of self. It seems appropriate to at least consider it to be potentially delusional thinking. As a mental health professional I feel inclined to assist any client based on empirically-supported methods. Humane respect for their personal right to self-determination is a fundamental basis for our association. A primary goal is to achieve a comfortable, psychological state at the onset of therapy. After achieving a stable state and provide caring, empathetic therapeutic treatment, I must consider that a deceptive acceptance of unsupported reality is inappropriate. The idea that professional practice must be obliged to ignore a reality from sense interpretation is not beneficial to the client. Such a position is not a basis of therapy. To progress in treatment in this manner is absurd. Or are we to ignore the adage of, "seeing is believing"?

Adding to derision and delusional progressions from our origins, most people in western civilization are ill-equipped to be self-sustaining. Only a very few individuals are responsible for the growing and raising of the food supply for the vast majority of the population. Granted there are those on small farms but this number has been presented, by one estimate, as being less than 10% of the U.S. land owners. If you ask a young child where a hamburger comes from chances are that they will identify a grocery store (or a fast-food chain) as the origins of their meat. Likewise, describing the proper procedures for planting and tending a crop of vegetables is not a known experience to many. I would be surprised if many urban inhabitants could provide insight into the essential duties associated farming and animal husbandry. I am certain that many would be too repulsed to engage in the slaughter of the meat that they consume. Additionally, they could expect to face being confronted by animal rights groups for doing so. This is an affront to a Creator who provided us with the bounty of nature with only our toil and attention required to harvest our food. This supports my arguments regarding our unstable status and the shaky ground that many people in our world presently occupying.

And not only are we ill-equipped to provide food for ourselves, the food that is consumed is a consequence of woman's entry into the workforce. In this instance it relates to diet and obesity. In my years as a child and adolescent, my mother was in the home. She made sure that we were doing what we were supposed to and completing homework after school hours. Further, with her present in the household, we had nutritious meals since she had the necessary time to address our needs. We had well-rounded meals with each food group represented. The meals were of sufficient quantities and quality to ensure our continued health. Now, with the mother and/or wife absent from the household this is not always possible. This is the basis for reliance on fast food for the family's nutritional needs. The advent of high-sugar, high-salt, and high-fat diets as the primary means to satisfy hunger has promoted the growth of restaurants and fast food chains in present culture. This is at the center of controversy concerning obesity. No matter how one tries to frame the topic of obesity, this is primary to the origins of the problem.

Along with a lack of adequate time to prepare those well-rounded meals that I was accustomed to as a youth; we now have unconsidered health issues from this role change. The result is mass-consumption of processed foods. All of those chemicals found in today's highly processed foods cannot be good for us!

An equally disturbing reality is the loss of recognition of the importance of the principles of accountability and responsibility in secular society. These two principles have been excluded from the expectations of our culture as a response to liberal left-wing attitudes that sees things absent these ideals. Their perception is that our world is to be considered based on interpreting "gray areas". This is where there is truly no absolute right or wrong, rather we have to overthink everything. We marginalize, minimize, excuse, deny, pervert, confuse, or avoid, but never assess blame or responsibility. Crime is not adjudicated to be accounting of the nature and full extent of the offenses. Rather, allows for a leniency that is not appropriate to represent the extent of the sociopathic criminal behavior is our response. A person's life is worth little in the present judicial system that allows for short sentences for the murder of innocents. We parole those who have perpetrated even the most heinous crimes based on overcrowding of jails. I don't conclude the relevance to our safety as associated with availability of money but, "Who am I?" This is the reality that fails to operate with accountability and being held fully responsible for their acts.

Along with this new social norm, people should not be personal responsibility is the new endorsement from liberalism. We do not hold people responsible for their own lives. Some do not securing their own resources legally or by work-related efforts to provide for their off-springs. The progressives and liberal-left see the answer to everything riding on securing more tax revenue. The source is from those who strive to be responsible and self-accountable. Our liberal social welfare machine then redistributes these monies to allow others to avoid the due diligence at self sufficiency (while attempting to buy happiness).

This lack of responsibility and accountability exists along with the idea that we, as a people, operate frequently with rights absent obligations. Law has legislated God from our lives as his existence threatens this notion of avoidance of obligation. As our government carefully delineates him from their operation, we have disassembled family as it was designed in our past. Instead, we include non-reproductive units as a legitimate family structure. The best interests of our children or elders are approached from an attitude of costs, convenience, and assessments of potential return. Vulnerable members of society are weighted in relation to actual, immediate threat to the needs priorities of others being realized. Should there be a perceived inconvenience which is assessed as difficult, then a consideration of the past or future provision from these vulnerable members is ignored.

The scriptural adage that a double-minded man is unstable in all his ways applies to our wanton disregard for value of spiritual guidance. We have reached a point when the sheer insanity over the lack of the use of reason has defined our world as insane on many levels. We had been previously acquired and refined over a 6,000 years history the importance to thinking through our situations to progress. The base arrogance of our hedonistic predispositions are overtaking our society as we convulse due to the lunacy of many unsupported positions. From both our institutions and from those who direct our society, the sheer madness is hard to fully grasp. Fundamentally, the words or concepts of evil and sin are unacceptable ways of referring to conduct. These Christian principles, previously considered accurate ways of understanding amoral practice are avoided. The acceptance of these previous considered amoral practices have exploded and are now supported and judicially-enforced. The fact is that society is no longer bashful about its behaviors, the conceit for our source is demonstrated so clearly that he cannot remain blind to it.

All of this has contributed to, and allowed for advancement towards, a state of anarchy. Divergent news casts point to upheaval throughout the world with ongoing riots and demonstrations of the masses in cities. Generally, the distress is associated with a lack of basic needs frequently not met. Usually, the attitude and perception is that government is responsible for their needs being met. This is in opposition to scriptural ideals of needs being met by their own ingenuity. A few individuals have more wealth than billions of their fellow earthly inhabitants. They fail to reinvest their money into the economy to provide work for the masses. Thus, many do not have an opportunity to be self-sufficient. Meanwhile, the average American is having needs (and wants) being met by government which depends on spending money that is not available.

The U.S. government continues to print money without anything of intrinsic value to support it. Further, we are being propped up by foreign governments who are providing us loans that we will not be able to pay when they become due. In short, there is a time bomb that is about to explode. The world will embrace a world leader who can get need met. Concurrently, he will usher in further erosions in liberty and morality. The people, operating primarily from a hedonistic attitude, will not care. These things have been foretold and the writing is on the wall. It is only those who are oblivious to scripture who fail to acknowledge the signs of this age. With no future beyond their life on this planet and engaged fully in living for today; they will ignore the obvious future that awaits them. If one points these circumstance out then they are summarily classified as a loon. Secular self-insularly comfort dismisses these concerns and denies the relevance of this belief. Excuses, insult, and other derogatory labels for those who disagree with their "progress" is the response. The reality is that this allows for a state that avoids for a harsh, critical self-assessment.

How does one know what future awaits them? There are some principles in operation to concluding this question for each of us. Using a couple pertinent principles on begins with one my dad shared with me often. There is always a payday; no matter how far into the future it may take there will invariably be a payday. Secondly, scripturally stated, a tree is known by its' fruits. It cannot produce both good and bad fruit although some will try to hedge on this point. Their counter is that some fruit is blighted while other fruit on the tree is good and juicy. The scriptures speak to being either good or bad but not both. The conclusion for this scriptural adages is that the tree producing bad fruit will be thrown into the fire as not worthy of saving. The obvious lesson from this second principle is that it we will be judged either good or bad. This denies present-day confusion resulting from "gray area" logic that suggests that being "kind of" moral and obedient will suffice. This returns us to the first point. If one is known by bad fruit due to disobedience, the payday will be eternal separation from God. Be aware, the kingdom of God has no suburbs. Either one resides within this city or in eternal darkness absent our Creator. Although some would argue these points, this explanation has been concluded based upon multiple readings of scripture. The inherent word reinforces that this is, indeed the case, and denial won't alter the reality for how it will end.

With an ended on this note, the reason for writing this book would be unclear. It would seem unnecessary to engage in the exercise of putting pen to paper. The central reality to all that we are human and doomed to fail, in many instances miserably. This failure, imperfection, and lack of purity requires us to be reliant on our Creator for both our reprieve and forgiveness. He provides with comfort while we continue to fall short. We are not all that. This denies the annoying attitude that is prevalent. Our errant imperfection bears acknowledgment with demonstrated humility instead of undeserved pride of self. We are desperately in need of forgiveness and must rely on the grace of God. We must continue to try to reach out to him for our salvation. That is the nature of our existence.

Further, accepting the Son and acknowledging our sin while asking forgiveness and dedication of our life from that day forward to him is essential. Lastly, a love of our source and his creation must occur to complete the requirements as I have come to understand his plan for our salvation. Even though I pray for us all to be aware of all of this, I resign myself to letting the person's ambivalence or dedication to God's instructions serve as basis for their demise. Ignorance, or defiance, will not be beneficial to our cause to be given mercy. Doing so will lead to having an awareness that we didn't have one of our better days when we have to give account of our lives.

It would be very much an error to not acknowledge that we all fail to live up to the expectations of our Creator and none are blameless. We are all in need of forgiveness. How we measure others will be equally weighed upon us in fair turn. So, I must again make clear that central to my purpose for writing this chronological listing of our ongoing fall from grace. This is a wake-up call for the reader to go about making straight the path and leaving this folly of self-emulation. I admit that it seems somewhat daunting-the task of remaining cognitively connected to God's plan on a daily basis. However, the alternative to exerting an ongoing effort is so displeasing that whatever accommodations are required should be made. So that this connection may occur, ensuring our continued self-preservation is primary to having a chance of correcting our world. The central problem is that many do not even care and don't see a need to be excused for their behavior. Our Creator is eager to draw us near to him. Instead, many see their behavior as permissible which is another way of saying that God has lied and does not expect anything specific of us. The reasoning continues that he really didn't mean what he has expressed per gospel print. Meanwhile, many dilute his commandments and admonishments to us regarding how to live and head forward to our own assured self-destruction.

I want to make it clear that I am a sinner and fall short of God's design. I am, in no means trying to suggest that I am better than others. I am trying to apply my lifetime of education, experience, and scriptural growth to the cause of preventing those who are concerned for their future from a detrimental fate. I am optimistic that hope infers that our future can be avoided. As Christ said more than once, "those who have ears hear". I have frequently used the following example as an explanation for the age old question regarding why we are here as well as what it is all about:

Life is nothing more than going to school. We are in a grade and must learn a lesson in order to be advanced to the next grade and lesson. If we don't master the material we stay in that situation until we do. We continue to learn lessons and continue to grow and succeed and finally graduate, or, we quit and experience failure for our lives. The lesson that must be learned is how to be obedient and develop a personal relationship with God. After all, would he want someone in his midst that you can't be in communion with? We must develop the insight to understand, accept guidance, and realize his hopes and wishes for us. We also need to truly come to appreciate him, what he has done for us, the world, and each other. The key to this entire exercise lies in the simple fact that God "knows our heart" and who we really are. This is the essence of the consideration regarding our place of eternity.

As to the purpose of living, it is to use the abilities that he has provided us with to their fullest extent to promote his kingdom in the hearts of man. Also, the experienced joy our God gains while he watches us going through those lessons and arrive at the point when we "get it" is the return he cherishes that made all that he has done worthwhile. We have come to truly be his, beyond his part in our design, and in spirit and truth. Finally, the love that we show to God is also required for our fellow human being. This will determine if we are held blameless or open to judgment. After all, our Lord gave us instruction to follow in order to have fulfilled all of the commandments. Our gratitude, love, acceptance, and honor of him will seal the deal. The greatest thing that any of us can ever hear is the words "welcome home, my true and trusted servant."

However, this theme of continued alienation of the created from the Creator requires examining the use of language by elements of liberal thinking to confuse attempts at rational awareness of our world. Many secular individuals claim that civilization has "progressing" thereby suggesting that we are improving our world situation. The thinking is that, each succeeding step of disobedience to our Creator, suggest a better life. The aspects to our progression that I have alluded to earlier in this chapter are seen by seculars as improvements to the culture. Somehow, it is inferred that we are better off than we were before when we valued family over property, life over convenience, and self-worth derived from honest personal effort to be self-sufficient. A step further, our improvements include identifying anyone who places value on scripture and notes transgression of secular society as mean spirited or ignorant. In these instances, secular people have been stated as saying they have a "problem with the person".

In reality, when scripture is quoted and secular individuals have a "problem" with the person, their disgust for God is demonstrated. Having a problem with God due to dislike of scripture, and the absolutist interpretation rendered, is not a particularly productive viewpoint. Undoubtedly, they will have their opportunity to express their complaints to the Creator at some point if one believes in a judgment. These errant feeling and attitudes about his thinking and expression will not endear them to him. They will be found lacking in reasoning to support their irreverent behaviors. Since God is not interested in our opinions, rather, in our compliance; we will be judged on what we have done and said. How we feel about his guidance and directions will be noted as it relates to our intentions and understanding our heart for him. Since they choose to demonstrate this character trait, they really seem likely to be on the short end of the stick so to speak.

Chapter Eleven

Conclusion--Doing the Right Thing

Ignoring New Age Fallacies

At the forefront of the demonstrated deterioration of our culture as projected in this book is the exercise of poor behavior. The issues of present-day society, and fundamental basis for these issues directly relates to the concept of change. The disproportionate importance that western culture places on ill-advised actions is insightful. These actions have dire consequences for us and many occur due to lack of insight regarding cause-effect from determination of benefit, absent later realized, destructive effect. Our rush to achieve ever-increasing luxury absent the base functioning to secure the desired benefits is embarrassing. All of these practices of societal development are associated with the central theme of change. Change is good, desirable, and necessary as a constant for a growing, thriving society is the official liberal-oriented party line.

This is at the core of many of the problems that plague us now and an examination of the detrimental effects of change follows.

In any age there are things that are determined to be in need of amendment, however this need to change lacks accurate consideration. The traditional values and beliefs which have essentially supported ongoing advancement have now been viewed as obsolete. This devaluation of cultural heritage has led to a point in our history when potential anarchy on equal with some of the darkest times in civilization has the potential to occur. The family is dissolved with a fundamental redefinition provided based on humanity, absent moral guidance. Our children are denied discipline for a fear that we will hurt their self-esteem while they lack positive modeling when parents are not present. Drugs are a multi-billion dollar business and scourge on society as pleasure pursuit has found fertile expression that causes extreme stress on many societal institutions. It is considered inappropriate to have accountability on practically any level. This has occurred due to a subjective sense of reality existence based on opinion instead of absolute, previously accepted expectations of conduct. Essentially, our evolved state has control and mastery over the populace and operates deceptively, based on their spin on facts versus objective reality. Many congenial people express that we lack freedom in a country that was based on spiritual precepts to design public policy. To be fair, a portion of our nation do love Christ and the Father and provide evidence that all of his creation is not in opposition to his hopes for us. They honor and uphold traditional values while adhering to time-honored practices. Although I wish otherwise, the problems are epidemic. Despite examples of strength and stability this epidemic can bring down all of that which has taken many generations to achieve. The accumulated advancements of our experiment in representative government may be overwhelmed by the few who do not share our ideals, traditions, cultural beliefs, or goals. A general lack of demonstrated obedience to our God is the overriding theme.

A consideration concerning people's lack of spiritually appropriate behavior can be traced to a simple factor. It is often easier avoiding the reality that we are immoral and that it will eventually matter. Rather than acknowledging and making changes to a behavior by being responsive to their conscience for what they know to be wrong, secular opinion depends on spiritual snippets to support disinterest. The common explanation that I have heard is that, "God loves all of us and everyone is going to heaven". If this were so, why are we here rather than just having everyone beamed up without any demonstrated respect for rules, authority, and values placed on us by scripture often attributed to God? Additional secularly expressed, delusional thoughts regarding spiritual reflection include, "it really doesn't matter, it isn't that bad after all, or others are much worse". This level of secular moralizing is not parallel to reality of spiritual prose or any understanding attained through study of God's word. Few readily accept themselves as immoral and even fewer will accept themselves and inappropriate in God's eyes. Instead, the invariable expression that "everyone is doing it" to avoid the reality of their indiscretions is muttered. Rather than experience personal discomfort with oneself, avoidance allows the practice of distraction to deny the quiet time to reach out and connect with our Creator. Other common practice include lashing out anyone who observes an impropriety or sinful behavior of that person. The unjustifiably offended secular avoids inward reflection that would undoubtedly lead to a crisis when they realize they really aren't the great one. In fact they are actually in the wrong although gray areas allow for mitigation of the sin.

Often the only instances where there is an attempt to reach out is in instance of misfortune or tragedy. The question becomes, "why it had to happen". In other instances, a favor or benefit that did not come with a prior personal relationship with the Creator is the cause for reaching out. Instead never-ending change to avoid the stability found with a relationship with our source occurs to chronicle our progress. The latest, new and improved, or needed change is our expression of the world we embrace as it relates to our interest in self and other people in preference for our origins. Fundamentally, we fail to acknowledge the need to heed his blueprint for life. The overwhelming result to pondering the secular behaviors regarding their spiritual association is that, essentially, they view this as they do their earthly behaviors. There will not be a negotiation, and compromise will not be involved. This is not about coming to a consensus. The old time adage, "the man with the gold makes the rules" represents the reality determining our inclusion in the kingdom. The basic avoidant nature dismissing efforts to engage in lifelong connection to our Father and the Son in preference for immediate interests is not even reasonable.

The central fact that is lost on present-day society is that change is not inevitable. It is not even always wise and appropriate. I know that this is lost on those who value change, however, believing in the necessity to do something with every moment does not equate with productivity. A difficult lesson is that sometimes we need to mark time and just allow what is to continue. As humans, there is a better than average chance that we will only makes things worse otherwise. What I have observed is an overwhelming demonstration of obsessive-compulsive behavior that requires people to account for their every moment. Something seems required to represent the passage of a given period of time. Enjoying each other's company and the blessings and bounties of God is worthy of our interests instead. Being subservient to him allows us to avoid pushing ahead with frequently poorly-planned and ill-conceived ideas from an inability to show restraint. It is not a bad thing to be obedient-he would not ask anything of us that would be detrimental to our well-being. His interest in us, as his children, has our well-being and longevity in mind.

Along with unending change there is an overwhelming tendency for extremism in our reasoned judgments. An example (one of many possible examples) is how we have went from housing mentally-ill individuals collectively to roaming the streets, sleeping over steam grates, and sit aimlessly in alleyways or subway stations. We view their use of park benches as available furniture and suffering through frigid weather as acceptable because they need to demonstrate their "individual freedom". Granted, treatment in previous years at many mental hospitals was reprehensible yet instead of reform, we go to the other extreme. Instead of demonstrating accountability and dealing with the mistreatment, we throw out the entire system in favor of release into society without considering that it is not really in our, or in the mentally-ill patients best interest to do so. In some cases, these individuals end up killing multiple innocents based upon delusional representations of reality. They would be better served with caring, empirically-based inpatient mental health treatment so as to safeguard both themselves and the public. There are other examples of demonstrated national policy trait of extremism of which I will only offer a few.

We provide money to those who claim that they need things. The idea is suggested that money will allow them to provide for their needs and ensure their happiness. An old adage is that "money cannot buy happiness". Our present-age sees this adage as inaccurate and out of date. The possession of things is considered to be more beneficial than a meaningful relationship to promote connection to our world. It is entirely possible that one of the most fundamental ills of modern society is the desire for money at all cost. This desire and compulsion surpasses the value to act with an honorable and dignified character in our personal affairs. The end has come to justify the means when the secondary gain of money is involved. Self-reliance and pride from honest effort become ignored when morals are discarded for the greed of money. This is, perhaps, the most flagrant form of extremism and leads to separation of the created and the Creator. I have always been allowed to live within my means since I made the decision to place a higher value on my relationship with my source than money. Finding solace with our spiritual life is in opposition to the pursuit of treasure. The one cannot be anymore removed from the other-gaining money in trade for losing our soul seems to allow for an obvious conclusion. Faulty reasoning serves as the foundation to our social programming with the guiding goal being providing money solely. Rather than address the more essential problem of a lack of connectedness to our Creator, our environment, and our fellow humankind. Greed is in!

We started out 50 years ago with a War on Poverty and invested in a welfare state. Today, we have as many or more people living in poverty than we did when we began. Trillions of dollars have been spent and for what? We took away the dreams and ambitions of entire generations of individuals and replaced it with programs to wit they flock to get "free stuff". In the process we lost the drive and incentive to invent and invest in America. (What never ceases to amaze me is how hard people work to avoid working while applying for benefits to circumvent work). Those who do strive for achievement and productivity are doing so to provide for over half of America that has preferred a program to personal ambition. A minority percentage of Americans fight our wars and suffer the injuries and mental disorders from combat out of a belief in the importance of serving their country. They attempt to honor and protect our values and traditions. Meanwhile, a majority percentage of the populace believes that a few dollars in donations to a veteran's cause is sufficient to account for a lack of personal sacrifice for our way of life. Unless one has served in the armed forces they cannot understand the insult that can be felt by small tokens that do not approach service to country. This does not meant that there are not some who do many great works for the benefit of our service members. Just most people offer trinkets and ignore the sacrifice that has been made by so many in our cemeteries who lived and died for a country founded on the faith in God as our source. This is America.

We, as Americans, boast about how we are the greatest nation on earth and most powerful as well. Reality is however quite different. We import more than we export and borrow to finance our social programs. Our liberal-minded politicians continue to ignore their own governmental agencies that yearly report that the government is spending in an "unsustainable" manner. If the middle-eastern countries would boycott America and not sell us their oil and oil- related products, we would be in a financial free-fall within one month. This is in spite of the fact that the United States produces massive amounts of oil and oil-related products. This is because we consume more than any other nation on earth of the world's resources. It is by such a significant margin that it serves as an embarrassment. Part of this consumption is evidenced by the purchase of trinkets from other countries that plot our downfall and wish us dead. These countries, in turn, use the money spent by American consumers to buy those trinkets to purchase our properties. They arm themselves to assault us when they determine that we have sufficiently succumbed to our own excesses while purchasing our means of production (factories). Point being, we lose the ability to make what we need and, essentially, will ensure our decline and demise.

And, we have become so self-serving that more than a few place themselves on the same level and same breath with our Creator. There is no consensus regarding an acknowledgement of his sovereign nature. We exclaim Happy Holidays rather than Merry Christmas so as to discount any celebrations of Jesus Christ's birth. After all, we don't want any atheist to be offended do we? The insolence has become so blatant that even religious people are harassed and civilly persecuted. Even nuns who are helping the less fortunate have come under liberal scrutiny. And, as a matter of national culture, narcissism and entitlement have become so much the norm that the common nature of the behavior is not even acknowledged as unusual. This mention leads to examples that we can all identify. For me it is the unsafe situation that one is exposed to every time they drive on the highways where many drivers acts suggest that reaching their own destination is not tied to ensuring safety of others also. There are mannerly drivers but it is becoming more common to see an absent any care for others rights or safety. In short, it is all about having their needs met as one gets the impression that if they don't accelerate they will be run off of the highway. It has so blatant, that being compliant with almost any signs or publically located instructions constitutes a burden to a measurable portion of those who use the services or facilities. This is perception that seems to be appropriate by my observations.

The bottom line is that it is not necessary to ignore, blast, or criticize those values and traditions that have been so much a part of the American landscape for centuries. Popular textbooks in the present-day classroom demonize our founders. Those who built our national institutions are portrayed as perpetrators of violence and mistreatment of others. The denial of reality that we live in a country which other nations envy due to our accomplishments is in practice. Our present state of liberalism denies that any other meaningful or significant milestones can equate with their personally perceived monopoly of the past 50 years. If we were to be honest, keeping ideals and values that have led to our success are not out of touch or old-fashion. These ideals are, in fact, timeless and never go out of style. What is really important is to keep alive the heritage that has served us all immeasurably. What has given us our success should lead us to understand that we need to "dance when the one who brought you". For most of our history the rest of the world has envied our governmental structure and our freedom to succeed. If we had not truly made something magnificent then why has the rest of the world repeatedly made the voyage to come here? They enjoy our way of life and seek citizenship while being provided economic support absent any expectations or requirements that those who are already citizens are required to honor?

My ancestor provided the treaties that provided the ideas and principles which our founding documents for our representative government are derived from. I feel a personal, special connection to our way of government that is hard to express to others as a result of contributions that are heart felt. Now I am disturbed by the efforts of modern-day, liberal-progressives who are dismantling the governmental structure by using fiat for governance. Equally, the development of a forth branch of government (federal agencies) is inexcusable. The formation of our system of government was based on my ancestor's belief that the people had a right to select those who would govern. Administrative agencies are making laws and ordinances which we are all drastically limited by as a consequence. We have not given legitimacy to their pronouncements as we did not vote them into the positions that they hold. Their actions are not derived from the consent of the governed is the simplest (and most direct) way I can state it. This expansion of the over-reach of administrative agencies (in order to bring more and more regulations to control our existence) is choking the life out of its citizens and paralyzing any attempts to function efficiently. The government has been sabotaged by liberal judge's decisions who, likewise, were no elected by the people. (I must make note that I believe that many, or most, judges are pious and honorable individuals who take our moral heritage into account. The harsh present reality is that the long term strategy of liberalism is now being fully felt with the few sabotaging the reputation of the many). These individuals deny the demonstrations of moral deference of state constitutions and state legislators acting on behalf of their citizens. The reflections of the people's will who attempt to remain compliant with their Creator are trampled. This is due to such an excessive legal hair splitting exercise that appears to be perverse, over-representations of insignificant distractions of limited legal value. Basically, this practice does not reflect my idea of common sense. Our politics, government, and judicial determinations have become one with the expression of liberalism as law, rather than being a position from which to form one of many alternative options for the governance. My question is, "Why do we wish to ingloriously defame our legacy by adopting European liberalism that is central to their present crises and shown as ineffective"? Is it possible that after all these years of our heritage, were we actually wrong, the world delusional, and preferring us to others as the place to bring your poor or realize your potential is undeserved?

The most repulsive aspect to this ongoing disregard for sensibilities involves having minor segments of society receiving attention to promote views and beliefs that are offensive to many. Our collective conscious is confronted with alternate and atheistic viewpoints which demand our acceptance and find support from secular, liberal legalism. I am perplexed how views shared by such a marginally numerical segment of society are provided with such attention. It bears mention that our Creator loves all of his creation and feels pain at every failure of character that results in turning their back on him. The problem is that it has not become enough to not judge others, now the legal code condones these behaviors and suggests that these behaviors are permissible. This is sending entirely the wrong signal to our source. It is one thing to avoid God's judgment by not judging others, it is entirely different to legislate in favor of what scripture suggests as unacceptable behavior. It is up to our Creator to judge these behaviors and I defer involvement in this controversy. I know my Creator's position without needing to elaborate what is self-evident. I have every confidence that his judgment will be consummate with his recorded prohibitions, otherwise God would be lying which is not reality. God does not lie. Nor will he say that defiance will be mitigated due to this new way of seeing the world known as humanistic liberalism. Without the saving grace of the Son's intervention, the results will be stark and severe.

Traditions such as our holidays are under assault by some misguided individuals who see any time-honored symbols in opposition to their beliefs. Our traditions become fair game to insult and attack as a result. Christmas is a derivative word-wise to suggest a celebration for the birthday or birth time of Christ. We can be fairly well assured (if we can trust the available research) that he actually was born in the early spring, or so many explanations provide. We have chosen to honor him by placing a yearly date for his celebration of birth and that is what is significant. An Atheistic group spent a large sum of money to display a sign in Times Square (New York City) during the Christmas season. They asked if Christ is even necessary as a part of the celebration of the season. As could be expected, some spiritually-deficient individuals eagerly joined in a demonstrated irreverent agreement basically devoid of any respectful behavior. This represents but one more example of why the writing of this text is important. The sheer, obscene expression of unmitigated insolence towards the deity of our Lord, who undeservedly suffered beyond any manner for our salvation in spite of our sin, is unacceptable by even the most accommodating standard. A push back is necessitated.

I do not have the exact statistics for these groups but it seems a safe bet to consider much less than 10% of the country are involved that hold these beliefs. Why do the liberal mainstream media, legalism, and political left-wing components of the country obsessively push these marginalizing group's agendas into the national discussion? The extensive coverage providing is not consistent with their comparative representation of the populace. What insane sense of promotion of tolerance forced the many to be antagonized by the few? We are required to coexist when, realistically, their expressed behaviors are an affront to our senses. Just what extent of enough is enough, the stench to our nostrils (to use a scriptural expression) has teased our nerves to their limits it seems accurate to say if I take seriously those who express their disgust rather than cower to the aggression exercised by these groups and their supporters.

So what is the answer? To chronicle the state of rebellion without providing a solution would be surrender to the ones who have an expressed desire to neuter our spiritual heritage and faith. The importance of a solution to address our state of separation from our Maker must include considering how to change our spiritual climate. It will prolong the time when penance will be required and give us an opportunity to even more extensively consider ways to reconnect with the values and beliefs that have reflected our roots. We must practice traits that will allow for spiritual living as an example to give pause and result in others realizing the validity of their God's ideas. Tolerance without giving legitimacy to immoral behaviors, patience without surrender to instant gratification, humility in acknowledging our sinful state, not judging to avoid being judged, grateful without material ambitions, faith that overcomes injustices, and love that is the source of all that is of our Creator, sum up a responsible attempt to influence our world.

I am sure that in the quiet moments of their lives, alternate lifestyles and atheistic beliefs realize that their way of living is not supported with spiritual representations attributed to our Creator. Within biblical text content support and a consideration as appropriate is not evident. A perceived rationale for their push for legal sanction seems to provide an opportunity for comfort. The belief seems to follow that legal permission will lead, at some point, to full acceptance by society. Their goal is to have others embrace their behavior although common spiritual and traditional cultural positions clearly failed to be favorable. No matter if a law sanctions the behavior or people say that they will not judge least they be judged, the behavior will ultimately incur a cost. Any attempt to dissuade the behavior only seems to mobilize those who find no fault due to a secular predisposition to push more. I ultimately accept that they will be called to question and not I. Their behavior and beliefs seem to be a millstone that will be the source of a final decision of their doing. We will be called to task as a nation for openly disobedience by legally sanctioning what God prohibits. So, besides the need to be clear in our opposition so as to be separated as sheep are from goats, those who fail to stand with God will receive their earned rewards. Clearly in our dissent, yet loving in our prayers, hope for mercy for them, that based upon scripture has a fate that awaits them due their behavior. We do this just as we should hope that others will pray for us to be rescued from our own indiscretions. As sin is sin without any one being more or less sinful than another indiscretion, we are all required to tread lightly.

We must be patient. If your views are in the minority nationally, within a few years, you will be back in vogue. Things operate in cycles and patience will be rewarded as we have policy corrections that address dysfunction. A truism is that approval allows for disapproval once approved operate unfettered for a time. Non-spiritual behavior is often fickle and patience will bear the storm from behaviors and policies causing current discord. We can only hope that awareness of our unstable state will shift to more spiritually considered behavioral mindset. The extent of, and full impact from recent examples of immorality have not currently been understood and what my work in this effort has personally revealed to my psyche is stark. My sincere, overwhelming awareness provides sad evidence that we have "crossed the Rubicon" and may be unable to renew a spiritually-based, civilized state of existence.

We must be humble. It is better to be brought to the head of the table by the host, than to be removed from the seat of honor for another. This is the story in scripture that addresses humility. Always know that what we are able to do was allowed by God's providence. We are unable to guarantee our survival, so give the credit to the one who makes all things work out to the advantage of the just. In spite of our personal acknowledgement of our individual greatness, we are really not worthy of the blessings that are bestowed on us by our Creator. It is by his pleasure that we have the many things we value. It is infinitely preferable to receive accolades by others than bestow platitudes on ourselves. Personal self-promotion is not becoming of a humble person so it is imperative to allow for our works to define us rather than our own self-describing adjectives.

We must be grateful. For everything that we have there are many who can only wish for the same. No matter how meager our possessions, many don't even possess that level of ownership. It has been said that I asked for shoes until I met the person who did not have any feet. This fairly clear adage supports the need for gratitude. It is important to seriously appreciate the little things in order to be prepared to accept bigger and better blessings. Appreciation allows us to have the mindset recognizes our Creator for the bounty he has bestowed on us instead of blowing our own horns. Giving thanks is vital in spiritual growth as it requires us to realize the sheer dependency that we have on God while keeping us humble as well.

We must practice faith. It is just as important to practice faith for the cultivation of hope for our future, is shields us spiritually while providing a modeled behavior for the observation by others who need hope for their own lives. We are part of a collective family and our faith, when our faith is practiced for all, demonstrates personal strength of character that encourages our brothers in Christ. The result is that one good deed leads to another one by "passing it on". We need stability in our lives, as does our society. When faith is active on a larger scale the results for our world include stability. As a people, we need to know that things will be alright. Good will prevail and faith helps give us purpose. Without faith in the future, and the subsequent hope that it engenders, the continuation of the humankind is not assured. Faith is the engine that provides the energy to go forth through a trial with the knowledge of its outcome without having any insurance in the outcome, and believe in ourselves to see any challenge through.

We must epitomize love in our every moment on the planet. No one knows the impact that a loving action has on the human condition unless they personally experience it. When there is a lack of love and there is injustice, the effects can be devastating. We realize the feeling that we get from the expression of love and in both the receipt and giving it is unequaled. It is one of the few things that I can think of that is as vital to give as it is to receive with such fulfilling experience that few things can compare to it. Scripturally it is said that God is love therefore when we love, we are in tandem with our God and truly doing his work. No matter what may occur on the planet, love is the single thing that can insure our survival. We will do what is necessary to secure safety and comfort to others when we love others first, and foremost, in our being.

These ideals represent important spiritual standard that may promote individual, and national, recovery. There are pragmatic steps that address the concerns impeding a return to prosperity and a moral basis of national standards. These steps can address pressing, and spiritually challenged, issues facing aspects America with a consensus that leads to resolution significantly righting serious and fundamental ills of society. They include:

Propose constitutional amendments that are voted on during a general election by all of the voters in the nation to settle the issues of gay marriage, abortion, and of balancing the budget.

It only seems proper our total voter-eligible populace should decide whether the biblical, spiritual principle of marriage as being between a man and a woman is our national tradition or if same-sex marriages are allowed to have legal support. Surveys have indicated that a majority of the population support placing conditions on abortion and the wishes of the majority should be honored. Having federal judges imposing their secular-will on generally spiritual peoples across the nation is not philosophically supported by traditional theory. My opposition to federal judge ruling comes from the philosophical traditions our nations embraced for significant part of our heritage. John Stuart Mills gave us the philosophy of utilitarianism which, succinctly expressed, determined the summa bona (most good) to be the basis of society. In short, the majority preferences equated with the greatest good of society. Although an elementary explanation, the present majority in America are forced to accept scripturally indefensible as well as personally repugnant values counter to our heritage. This is a means of being denied the reasonable exercise of the promises exposed by our founding documents and have been able to become entrenched due to contortions that are counter to the common sense of the majority. This determination by popular vote is from which the government derives is legitimacy. Finally, our federal debt is a paramount concern to many. It has been estimated that all tax revenues received from west of the Mississippi River are used solely to satisfy the interest on our current debt and, if so, this is incredible. As realistic as it seems that our government would realize the obligation to its citizen to demonstrate austerity in the nation's fiscal dealings, it seems that only the participation of the citizens to determine the requirement for fiscal responsibility will ensure that it occurs. We should approve a constitutional amendment for a yearly balanced-budget as well.

Sign into law a debt reduction plan which requires yearly reductions in the national debt by a predetermined amount annually and included in the yearly budget.

It is not feasible to expect the massive debt to go away overnight. We have amassed an amount that can only be chipped away at so that a systematic approach to the debt seems appropriate at, say, an approximate $ 333 billion dollar yearly payment towards the principle of the debt. At this rate by approximately the 51st year we would achieve total solvency, absent debt.

Enforce our drug laws and avoid attempts by law enforcement at the federal level from decriminalization of any drug sales or of the legalization of cannabis.

My professional experience as a supervised psychologist, when interviewing felons for classification and reviewing their criminal record has a reoccurring experience. Practically 9 out of every 10 cases directly, or indirectly, included drug in commission of felonies. Cannabis was the first used, and consistently reported drug first experimented with. The ages of 13 to 16 years as the beginning, routine use was universal and represented the gateway drug. More and more extensive use, of various mind-altering substances almost always followed. The use of cannabis began the process of addiction in most instances, and foreshadowed serious drug addiction leading to crimes associated with securing the resource to continue the habit or making poor choices while intoxicated by drugs.

Only a foolish individual would say that cannabis is not a major problem. Firsthand, I have witnessed the lack of motivation and interest in productivity associated with cannabis use. Finding a source to acquiring the drug, socializing the event of consumption, and eating followed by sleeping represents the usual day of use. This does not leave much time to attend to the responsibilities and obligations that represent present-day realities. Further, I would not feel safe having someone who is intoxicated working beside me. My personal concerns for safety may be compromised by altered, negatively affected movements and decisions. Innocent enough as it is in the life of a teenager, as scripture states, when one becomes a man they put aside their childish things. Even though many of us have knowledge of this experience, at the point of adulthood we are required to act responsibly. Personal obligations include contributing to society, our own families, and demonstrated respect of moral expectations that prevent our embarrassment from foolish actions.

Require universal military service. This ensuring adequate national defense and ends dependence on a few individuals to defend us. It would provide vocational skills training so that we would have more skilled citizens after discharge from the service. Individuals who could not meet physical requirements for military service would serve on public works projects or assisting in low-service areas. At the conclusion of the mandatory national service, based upon a points system, they may be eligible for financial assistance for college or vocational school training. At present, Pell Grants are available to all who meet financial need guidelines without having provided any contribution to the country.

These just mentioned suggestions represent pragmatic, common-sense answers in consideration to resolve problems of national impact for the people. At present, secular progressives with non-spiritual agendas control our national will without the majority wishes predominating for public policy. The future security of our nation requires financial stability based on sound, disciplined reasoned practices. Senseless spending, frequently tied to coalition building for political capital to assure continued control, does not honor taxpayer contributions. Benefits to support dependence tied to entitlement is unspiritual, irresponsible, and lacks popular support. The few have control over the levers of control and are manipulating the voters through social spending to ensure continued political support. As it currently stands, we are being pushed by a small, but vocal, minority opinion that feels that they know better what we want and need than we do. A response is necessary to reestablish the priorities of the majority of Americans. Our future survival as a nation and as individuals, hangs in the balance without guarantees of success over the issues that affront us at the present time.

In closing this discussion the closest approximation to be drawn of present American life involves a comparison between the behaviors of secular progressives and the biblical explanation Christ's intervention at Gergesenes. After Christ had transferred the evil from the possessed person to the swine they ran. Being in close proximity to the shore, the swine herd ran headlong into the sea and drowned themselves. They made no attempt to survive, instead, the herd purposefully and straightaway guaranteeing their own terminal demise without a fight. Progressive appear to be so committed to an agenda that is lacking in spiritual support, amoral if compared to biblical, Judeo-Christian values, and so out of the mainstream on various issues in opposition to majority opinions of these controversies that they don't seem to understand their delusions will spell doom to us all unless we basically flee. From a pragmatic assessment, they are running headlong to their demise while including the majority with them. Meanwhile, they have dismissed any traditional ideals and ignoring our protests with the eminent dissolving of our present social and political system included in the grand design. In a time past, we demonstrated a dependence on morality and values promoted by scriptural prose and now they have been distorted beyond retrieval.

This is not a comparison about any segment of the American population being equated with swine. Instead, it represents an observation comparing two groups with essentially the same inability to responsibly consider their own survival. We, as individuals and a nation, need to heed this parable. We must realize that the continuation of the American way involves continuations of a distinctive tradition. We cannot repaint the national experience absent our origins as something new and somehow not connected to its' past. We need not be ashamed or demeaning of our heritage. Our proud past as a safe haven for those who wished to worship the God of their forefathers with truth and light tells of a people who were principled with values and definite purpose. The present state of our country attempts to deny this and insert a philosophy alien to our history.

The present day use of "black" or "white" to frame issues by claiming discrimination as a tool, commonly, for avoiding the more important related fact of popularity being the benchmark for acceptance. In spite of denial, minority positions are accepted as policy and law at the expense of majority opinions often. Rather than respect the wishes of the masses, political policy rewards those who have pushed their agenda on the majority and allowed to exist due to lack of self-felt threats that these minority views are perceived to have. Face it, the facts of life are that the majority opinion on issues should have primacy in decisions that become policy. Why has the majority come to a point when they deny themselves this privilege because of the left-wing, liberal establishment that tries to shame them as a tactic that basically makes the discussion an emotional reasoned event minus rational component to support with data and hard facts. Insulting labels are used as a means of describing their opponents as actual discussion of the issues would not turn our favorable for their interests. As an example of liberal left-wing methods related to distraction and deflection for avoidance of substantive discussions consider this. The term "racist" is often used primarily as a response to those who fail to accept those policies and programs that are helpful to the minority groups in society. The disgruntled fail to realize that actual reasonable, genuine lack of shared interest or choice is the basis for opposition to the idea at controversy. The use of what I have previously referred to as "word salad" is at issue here with emotional reasoning diverting from rational discussion and attempting to shame or insult another as a calculated tactic to gain an advantage.

I have never met a parent that wanted their children to grow up to be a drug addict, get involved in criminal activities, or live a homosexual lifestyle in the time that I have lived. I have heard parents state that they hope that their children would have good health or financial abundance. Others wish for success without particular qualifications while others express hopes for their happiness. However, none of these other circumstances were ever favorably considered in my discussions with them. This does not mean that there may be a parent who is OK with these behaviors. Just that I haven't met one thus far. However, presently the national preoccupation with "political correctness" retards frank talk. Nothing can be discussed candidly or risk earning the label "hater". The common man just shrugs their shoulders while boisterous, loud liberal voices cause many to cower in spite of demonstrated arrogant disrespect. Traditional views and attitudes seem to cause extensive distress and result in severe attacks as a strategy to surrender to liberal opinions. Further, those who are representative of the mentioned categories are permitted to be unaccountable. They oppose majority expressed legislative wishes for their society and actually have their views have primacy in legal development. The screams of the minority have drowned out the majority opinion wishes.

In reality, the success of the liberal agenda is honoring the adage of having the squeaky wheel getting the grease. In practice, it represents a sell out on beliefs for the benefit of avoiding confrontation. Maybe some do not see the value or importance to fight those whose beliefs and values they know to be the reverse of our tradition because they just want to get along. Those ideals that have formed and sustained us are fair game though due to the practice of avoidance so as not to cause a scene. Defending what is important to us doesn't seem to be a priority. If one can just go to work, get their pay, satisfy their financial obligations, and have a few bucks left to have a good time then life is good. Or, in reality that is how it plays out for many who just want to avoid any controversy.

In essence, there is a lack of responsibility for actions that include facing tough tasks of calling out those who are an offense to our sensibilities. The reality is that few statistically are identified as being primarily interested in policy that is consistent with scriptural values. The idea is that money talks and all else walks. Evidence of this would exist if one considers that should taxes climb, then people will mobilize. In comparison, God can take care of himself seems to be the final word when plain expression occurs. It is deemed easier to ignore the previously considered, blatant immorality and hedonism that threatens to consume the national consensus. One nation, under God, indivisible, as within the guise of the pledge of allegiance isn't the common experience for the generations providing middle age direction to the country. The value to this ideal has been lost in much the same fashion as if it were an ancient relic for inspection based on curiosity. This means, in essence, that the spiritual moral compass of the free world is coming to a point when it loses its' flavor and will be good for nothing but to be tossed out and trodden under foot as the scriptural salt adage suggests.

It does not end there. By failing to support and nurture ideals that are the basis of our traditions and institutions, we will lose something even more vital. The soul of the individual and the collective soul of the nation, cannot sustain itself when it loses sight of its sense of reason. The present state of society is evidenced by name-calling and disparaging of individuals instead of pertinent discussion of issues based upon logic or the application of spiritual-based principles and ideals. If someone disagrees with the person, or when a person serves to be a threat to their power base or their belief system, then they accuse them of something that is little more than false witness. In an honest definition, it is more accurately identified as a lie.

Further, they pervert the legal system by piling on lawsuits against anyone who disagrees with them to silence dissent and sensible common sense understanding from scriptural prose. There is no regard for legitimacy of the legal actions as the motivation is to make anyone who objects suffer seems appropriate. If they can ruin the person financially while they provide their legal defense, then they have accomplished the objective. People seek to avoid speaking out to obvious injustice or perceived immoral behavior least they be ruined by a special interest group that seeks publicity and promotion of their agenda. The objections of those who must endure what they perceive as immoral and offensive practices do not receive legal standing. We are promoting ill will towards each other in direct violation to the most basic of spiritual values; that being to love one another. Instead of being a blessing to each other, the goal is to afflict the spiritual rather than self-assess general lacking in behavior. All I would suggest is that we would strive to be in compliance with God's guidance and expectations and avoid attempting to ignore or pervert his plan for our life on this planet and for the time to come. The ultimate result of this present abuse of judicial proceedings appears to me to be the dissolution of free speech. As a veteran who served to defend the right to speak frankly, I feel that failure to be provided this opportunity is the end to the idea of rights to express moral outrage. The contortions made to legal precedent make this consideration a possibility that most don't even realize is a near reality. Further, interpretation of the intentions of our founding fathers is so flawed in many instances that it is a blatant disrespect for our heritage as a nation dependent on the Creator for our legal and social mindset. Ultimately, the activists succeed due to the absence of money to protect the scripturally-bound individuals that do not possess resources to confront the financially viable and well-managed, liberalism-based activist organizations.

Consider this. Secular individuals do not value spiritual principles with any like importance by those led by the spirit rather than by the flesh. This has consistently been my experience. If there is no heaven and God does not have a reward for the compliant servant, then the secular person cannot be ridiculed for their demonstrated, unspiritual lifestyles. In short, what would be the motivation absent a personal desire to act with a personally-perceived "goodness"? On the other hand, as I believe that heaven exists and a set of parameters that must be met to be allowed to spend eternity there. It seems reasonable that the lifestyle necessary for acceptance includes spiritually-acceptable behavior. Can anyone gamble that there is no hereafter? If so there is no need to be mindful of our behavior, why has civilization always required expectations for conduct? Further, do we just want to live "in the moment" without regard to an eternal existence? In order to make this question clear and obvious, consider this. As you watch a cigarette smoker take a drag from a cigarette and then exhale a cloud of smoke. As you watch it travel it will go out into the air for a distance that may be as much as 20 to 30 yards. Then it dissipates and vanishes. This seems to be the easiest way to describe the scriptural adage that states that our lives are but a vapor, then gone. Further, understand that scripture states that our last breath on earth is our first breath in eternity and the basic comparison becomes clear. Eternity has an established beginning with the last breath as a human on earth and continues without end. As simple as I can make it, should you concentrate on the cloud of smoke, or have a preference for eternity? That truly is the central question to determine if this work, or any work on spirituality, will coercing someone to live a spiritual existence or not. Can you allow yourself to discover after your time on Earth is over that you should have lived by spiritual principles and in obedience to your Creator? Or, is man your god and science your religion? If so, you can accept yourself as just a descendent of an ape with this as your reality, absent God. Choose wisely.

Summary: Who Really Needs Who?

It is important to understand the approach for interpreting scripture that was then applied to give reason to my arguments for the case of God and his relevance to our future. Students of scripture usually interpret the spiritual text based on either an absolutist or an allegorical position with these alternate variations of applications leading to reasoning that may be counter at times. The majority of the determinations about what I have presented as detrimental to our existence and morally unsound comes from an absolutist position. To support this interpretation, I suggest that it is not acceptable to behave in a manner that is outside the bounds of God's commandments or pronouncements which are literally expressed. The inspired words of God are very clear. This is my position for an absolutist conclusion in their interpretation. Things appear to be as the adage states, black or white so to speak, in the way they are written. I do not provide an opinion of the intentions of my Creator as he has expressed his wishes without uncertainly or excuses to justify a lack of compliance. Things appear clear with an elementary command of language that is sufficient to alleviate any attempts of perverting the literal print of the texts from which the principles are derived. As is a common present-day expression that makes my point; "it is what it is".

We would not even be required to have a discussion about whether it is absolutist or relativist were it not for the age-old argument over initial absolutist interpretations of scripture versus the later theorized allegorical interpretations of those texts. Some will argue that things are said but not meant as they are stated (allegorical). This is only occasionally feasible as a way of considering scriptural prose when history or custom is in application or provides a context to a story or principle in the considered text material. Absolutist, who are scriptural purist, will reply that it only rarely the case that it isn't meant as it is stated, certainly not permissible to stray significantly from translations. Usually nothing more and nothing less is preferred when considering scripture. An obvious example of allegorical interpretations is to consider that Jesus did not necessarily mean we were to actually count the number of times we forgave someone until reaching the product of 70 times 7 (490) then, withhold forgiveness afterwards. It is generally acknowledged that we must not fail to forgive those who sincerely seek it.

Unfortunately, those who seek to argue questionable or outright immoral positions cling to allegory to excuse, minimize, or dismiss their transgressions and repugnant lifestyles. This has the results of making use of this technique ill-advised with reasonable allowance for disagreement not possible. Even worse, those who lean on allegorical connotations for common Christian ideals based on scripture often twist the text to defend behaviors that are so clearly described elsewhere differently that the attempted distortion that it argued is obvious. An accurate representation of scriptural prose based on consideration of the full text requires considerable study and reflection. Inevitably either inspiration or an awareness of an obligation to change occurs. This is the essential reason that those who chose deliberate preference for secular beliefs are less likely to exercise an interest in scripture. The uncomfortable realities from spiritual awareness fail to support their behaviors leading to an unfavorable knowledge regarding the undesirable future for a soul absence its origins.

An additional consideration involves present-day opposition to this absolutist presentation exists as a consequence of science, in practice, taking on the status as a religion with man as god. Presented spiritual explanations dispute man's preference for science which is based on research for proof or disproving ideas. Only with research to support scriptural prose that explains God's side of the story is proven validity by research are his conclusions accepted. Instead, the demonstrated attitude is that man is the primary entity to determine what is factual due to the evolved state of humanity with its science. The primary function of science (research) involves confirming or refuting an idea or concept. The thing under consideration is expressed in the form of a null hypothesis. This is a hypothetical statement of what is believed to be truth. Every outcome of research is either an acceptance of the null hypothesis or a rejection of the null hypothesis. The accuracy of the hypothesis is based on a numerical probability called a level of significance and indicated whether the data results support the hypothesis. (In other words, the probability that the hypothesis is really accurate). Typically, this level of significance, or probability that the results of the research are significant, is set at either 98% or 95%. It is never identified as 100% or identified as absolute truth.

In short, there is no absolute, undeniable true finding, rather a close approximation to total truth. For the average person who does not know these principles associated scientific theory of approximate truth versus the absolute fact of scripture. To most, science is the preferential choice for facts in a secular society. The expressed, infallible scientific expertise of man is revered throughout the academic experience with public embrace avoiding allowance for comparative worth of God who has been excluded without any opportunity to compete for the minds of his creation. We prefer a reality of less than 100% true and a science that allows for exceptions and uncertainly rather than our source. This ignores the legitimacy for a God who has provided scripture based on certainty and expressed with absolutes for conduct. There is no expression of probably in scripture, exact expectations avoid confusion that would otherwise allow spin. In order to remove any secular arguments for preferential status that advance scientific findings as evidence of man as god, consider that constant revisions of previous "facts" due to a continually improved understanding of the item being examined are a common occurrence. Any possibility that could reflect this embarrassing ineptitude of our secular world are hidden so as not to diminish our perceived greatness by exposure out in the open. Humble character would acknowledge that this is further evidence of the corruptible nature of human intellect that needs God. So, as an end result, the present age functions with science where there is no total, indisputable certainty with smug comfort. The end result being that people act based upon corruptible human perception constituting a close approximation to reality, rather than on an absolute certainty. And, in the present, most people base their secular future on the age of science to view their reality and provide their guidance in preference to their Maker.

So do we need God and does he need us? We are the created and he is the Creator. Notice the capitalization of Creator versus the lower case assessment of our identity as the "created". That should provide some degree of certainty that we are subservient to him. News flash, the created is not all that! It denies rational thought to say that when someone invents or makes something that they are not hopeful for its success. Anyone who has made anything tends to have a certain degree of pride in the development of it and even more so when it produces a positive response or aspect based upon its' being. I believe our Creator is no different. He wants for us to produce great things while he has our best interest in mind and he is engaged in ensuring our success and opportunity to thrive within the environment he has created. It goes without saying that when something is created patience is exercised to give it every opportunity to produce. However, our Creator has cut his losses before with the Biblical flood and is not above doing so again if things don't begin to operate in the manner for which he has prescribed for us.

Scripture compares man with "dirty rags" and states that "none are worthy". This seems pretty clear and we are not able to ensure our eternal salvation absent the Son (who stated that no one can get to the Father except through the Son). It appears to me to be asinine for anyone to even think that they are able to be accepted based on themselves. Our basic human state defines our dependence from which we cannot overcome based on our own works. When it gets to a state of society when we see ourselves without the additional consideration of being subject to and dependent on God, then we have served to place our continued existence in jeopardy. That is essentially where we are as a society, as a nation, as well as of our present world experience. It is necessary for us to face reality. Truth is we are essentially of limited utility and our only value is what our Creator places on us. For us to see ourselves individually, or other specific individuals, as worth of emulation or idolizing is indeed foolish. Only God matters in the final analysis and our ignorance to that reality, while placing man as the basis of mutual interest, seems so idiotic to me that I can't fathom what is going on inside the heads of what I perceive to be a significant portion of the population. Further, many individuals interest is gained because of appearance, money, material gain, intoxicants, status, or power and this is the hallmark of secular mainstream ideation. The last call appears to be in progress with the train leaving the station and everyone behaves as if there will always be a redeye so not to worry. What I have been confronted with by spending years to consider the information and put to print this awareness leads me to a conclusion that service will soon be terminated. Ultimately our world may either end in a blast of atomic energy or when the footprint of the Son rests on earth. For now, if we realize that our continual existence will be assured by turning from our sinful ways and face our Creator with obedience and praise; then we may continue for a time longer. He is all of that-not us.

For our part, does the Creator need the created? Not hardly. However, there is one thing that he gives us and that is free will. We can give a good accounting of ourselves with demonstrated love for God due to what, who, how, where, and why he has created us and our world. Our existence as well as the provisions which we have, in some cases, has been squandered, wasted, and destroyed. We need him and depend on his benevolence to continue life on this planet. Now everything revolves around being "fun" and, if it is not, many fail to demonstrate an attention span beyond an unfocused glance. Why he has allowed such leeway to ignore, pervert, or alter his directions to us while demonstrating tolerance in spite of our disrespect is beyond my understanding. I am very grateful for this being the case. He must epitomize the very essence of patience and love to endure our affronts to his wishes for us. After all, there is nothing that he has commanded for us to do that is not in our best interests for guaranteed survival and ability to flourish.

How can we begin to understand and fathom his design for our best interest? I don't believe that we realistically claim to know his intentions, considerations, or rationales for our design. So, why don't we just go along with his plans for us? It doesn't make much sense to ignore what he sees as in our best interest and continue to assume that the created knows better than he. There really isn't any defense that humankind can provide to justify our insolence that is the trademark of society, over the past centuries, and the time for retribution will draw near and we will be oblivious to its' arrival until it is really too late. I shudder at the tribulations that have been described in scriptures; it seems that even the warning of the severity of these things is insufficient to garner attention or fear that would activate obedience. In this regard, most people don't know what is in scripture, don't feel that they have time to find out, and really don't care although they will ultimately pay a price that is ultimately final.

It is very important to understand by each and every one of us that God means what he says. He didn't have a thought that this might be the way it should be or that it is alright to disagree. He is clear and direct about his pronouncements with no wiggle room for anyone to try excuse away their sin in opposition to his guidance. This is a serious problem for those who choose to disobey him and he will not take it lightly. One of the greatest disservices that we can do to each other is to try to interpret his words out of context or to alter the flavor of his prose. Those who choose to disobey must clearly understand that they will be held accountable. This represent a sentiment that is not observed in present-day thinking as accountability is avoided. When he said to multiply and be plentiful he meant just that, not that we could wean out those who were not planned or live a lifestyle that did not allow for this to occur. He stated that we were to love one another and not be a stumbling block but the world continues to be a dangerous place. There will come a time when God will fail to continue to endure our insolence. Those who do not take him at his word and obey, will pay a price that can only be avoided by the grace found with the advocacy of the Son to the Father on our behalf. The only problem with this is that many argue against the divinity of Christ and get angry for the mention of his name.

How can they have a right to expect his intercession at the time of trial as scripture refers to him as our advocate to the Father on our behalf?

Each of us has gifts that are wasted unless they are shared for the mutual benefit of all. Scripture speaks of this fact as well and is clear regarding our obligation to share these gifts with others to honor God by their use. I feel that I am vindicated with my source having exerted this effort as a gift to my world in testimony to my Creator. I can never do enough for he who has done so much that we fail to appreciate or deserve (along with his Son). This offering of efforts can never begin to recompense his unfathomable love for me and for all of those whom I pray will employ common sense to wake up and smell the coffee. I hope that I have supplied a worthy argument towards the recognition of our cumulative need for a change of course for society to delay calamities brought on by our own noncompliance. I am but one singular individual, and am not worthy as a sinner for the task that this book has undertaken. I apply print to the page in the hopes that some will be allowed to avert negative connotations for themselves due to our mutual poorly-advised indiscretions. It is up to each of us to individually arrive at a course of action (if we choose to do so at all) in order to alter an otherwise negative outcome. I can only hope that some will find cause for concern and take this text as a call to avoid an unpleasant experience that is of such a magnitude that any alterations necessary to avert their experience are justified. As always, may God continue to bless each of us with his grace, mercy, and love as he has faithfully done for so long now.

Finally, a question asked of my clients involved an examination of their perspectives during a counseling session concerns if the glass is half-full or half-empty. A likely perspective that many may come to believe to be accurate regarding the picture that I have presented of our world is that the glass is practically empty. Based upon completion of the reading of this book, I hope the reader will feel led to personally assess their relationship with our mutual Father and Son. Then take those steps deemed necessary after reflection on the content provided. I have found that the true test of knowledge is not from the study but from the successful application of what was read and considered. What I have understood in providing therapy is that once the onion is peeled down to its core, the reality of the person's life that is necessary to consider becomes known. This is the strategy used to hopefully lead the reader to be required to face a reality that our civilization's evolution, absent the one who is most important (our God) is in peril. And, considering what I perceived as the present days of evil that will invariably end with those who fail to honor their source finding themselves arriving to the abyss.

NOTES

NOTES

NOTES

NOTES